CW01346246

Why can't computer books be easier to understand?

Not all of us want to become computer professionals, but we do want to have fun with our computers and be productive. The *Simple Guides* cover the popular topics in computing. More importantly, they are simple to understand. Each book in the series introduces the main features of a topic and shows you how to get the most from your PC.

Simple Guides – No gimmicks, no jargon, no fuss

Available in the *Simple Guides* series:

The Internet	Internet research
Searching the Internet	Building a Website
The PC	Using e-mail
Office 2000	Putting audio and video on your Website
Office XP	Writing for your Website
Windows 98	Dreamweaver 4
Windows Me	Dreamweaver MX
Windows XP	Flash 5
E-Commerce	
Digital cameras, scanning and using images	

A simple guide to
Photoshop 7

Joli Ballew

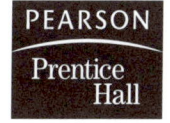

PEARSON
Prentice Hall

Pearson Education Limited

Head Office:
Edinburgh Gate
Harlow
Essex CM20 2JE
Tel: +44 (0)1279 623623
Fax: +44 (0)1279 431059

London Office:
128 Long Acre
London WC2E 9AN
Tel: +44 (0)20 7447 2000
Fax: +44 (0)20 7447 2170
website: www.it-minds.com

First published in Great Britain 2003
© Pearson Education Limited 2003

The right of Joli Ballew to be identified as the author of this work has been asserted by her in accordance with the Copyright, Design and Patents Act 1988.

ISBN 0-130-39910-8

British Library Cataloguing in Publication Data
A CIP catalogue record for this book can be obtained from the British Library.

All rights reserved. No part of this publication may be reproduced, stored in a retrieval system, or transmitted, in any form, or by any means, electronic, mechanical, photocopying, recording or otherwise, without prior permission of the publishers or a licence permitting restricted copying in the United Kingdom issued by the Copyright Licensing Agency Ltd, 90 Tottenham Court Road, London W1T 4LP. This book may not be lent, resold, hired out or otherwise disposed of by way of trade in any form of binding or cover other than that in which it is published, without prior consent of the publisher.

Screenshots reproduced by kind permission of Adobe.

10 9 8 7 6 5 4 3 2 1

Typeset by Pantek Arts Ltd, Maidstone, Kent
Printed and bound in Great Britain by Ashford Colour Press, Gosport, Hampshire

The publishers' policy is to use paper manufactured from sustainable forests.

Contents

Introduction . . . .*xii*
About the author xiv

1 Introducing Photoshop 1

What is Photoshop? 2
Cutting through the jargon 3
What are pixels? 3
What is resolution? 4
What are paths? 5
And never the twain shall meet? 7
Exploring the interface 7
Using the Toolbox 7
Using the Options bar 11
Using the Menu bar 12
Using the palettes and the Palette Well 13
More fun stuff with palettes 18
Palettes available from the Options bar 20
Summary 22

2 Enhancing photos 23

Opening a photo 24
Using the Open command 24
Using the File Browser 26
Acquiring an image from your scanner 28
Connecting a digital camera to your PC 29
Choosing the right view 30
Using the Zoom tool 31
Using the Hand tool 34
Display size, image size and file size 35
Adjusting the picture information 35
Making automatic adjustments 36
Working with brightness and contrast 36
Changing the hue and saturation 39
Tweaking the colour levels 40
Creating instant photonegatives 45
Minding the History palette 45
Saving your work 46
Summary 47

3 Editing photos .49

Making a selection .50
Using the Magic Wand .50
Using the Lasso tool .53
Processing your selection .55
Transforming your selection .58
Blurring, sharpening and smudging .61
Dodging, burning and sponging .63
Cropping .64
Changing the colours .66
Using the Eyedropper .66
Using the Paint Bucket tool .68
Using the Gradient tool .71
Feathering .74
Cloning .75
Summary .76

4 Creating art .77

Opening a canvas .78
Selecting the colours .80
Drawing lines .83

Using the Pencil tool 83
Picking a paintbrush 85
Erasing 88
Drawing shapes 90
Adjusting the size 95
Summary 97

5 Modifying paths 99

A quick refresher 100
Drawing with the Pen tool 101
Using the Path Selection tool 105
Using the Direct selection tool 106
Rasterising paths 107
Summary 109

6 Mastering layers 111

What is a layer? 112
Introducing the Layers palette 113
Creating and destroying layers 115
Showing and hiding layers 117
Locking and unlocking layers 118
Copying between layers 120

Linking layers 121
Grouping layers 122
Merging layers 123
Flattening the image 124
Summary 124

7 Using layer commands 125

Creating fill layers 126
Creating adjustment layers 129
Aligning, arranging and distributing 132
Adding layer styles 136
Applying shadows and glows 139
Bevelling and embossing 141
Changing the global light 143
Creating layer masks 143
Working with blending modes 145
Summary 149

8 Adding type 151

Using the Type tool 152
Comparing Point Type and Paragraph Type 154

Adjusting type properties 156
The Character and Paragraph palettes 157
Other type options 161
Warping type 161
Rasterising type 164
Summary 165

9 Using filters 167

What are filters? 168
Targeting selections and layers 168
Applying filters 169
Getting painterly 169
Adding distortion 173
Playing with light 177
Trying textures 180
Tips and tricks 182
Summary 184

10 Printing, saving and Web-readying 185

Printing your work 186
Setting up the page 186
The Print dialog box 188
Setting print options 193
Printing 193
Saving your work 195
Setting preferences for saving files 198
A few words about file formats 198
Exploring common file formats 200
Saving in Photoshop file formats 201
Optimising for the Web 203
Using the Save For Web command 204
Summary 211

Appendix 213

Creating Web pages in Photoshop 214
Creating a Web page using the Web Photo Gallery command 214
Summary 218

Index 221

Introduction

Welcome to *A Simple Guide to Photoshop 7.0*! If you are looking for the fastest and easiest way to become familiar with this program, you've come to the right place. This book is perfect for everyone new to Photoshop, and will enable you to get up and running as quickly as possible.

Photoshop is a complex and multi-faceted program; in order to understand its functionality and make best use of its capabilities, you've got to start at the beginning. I shall begin, therefore, by introducing some basic terms before diving right in to Photoshop 7.0's interface – the Toolbox, menus and palettes. Before you even finish Chapter 1, you'll be ready to work!

In this book, I'll teach you how to open and work with photographs, enhance them using automatic adjustments, and tweak their colours and hues. You'll learn how to select parts of photos and move them to other images, and add effects to images too.

You'll learn to create artwork using Pencil and Pen tools, brushes, and by using paths. You'll learn about layers and layer commands, adding text, using filters, and creating Web pages. You'll also learn how to print and save your work, and learn a little about file types along the way. When you are finished with this book, you'll be well on your way to becoming a Photoshop 7.0 expert.

Conventions and icons

Throughout the book we have included notes, each of which is associated with an icon:

These notes provide additional information about the subject concerned.

These notes warn you of the risks associated with a particular action and, where necessary, show you how to avoid any pitfalls.

These notes indicate a variety of shortcuts: keyboard shortcuts, Wizard options, techniques reserved for experts, etc.

About the author

Joli Ballew is a full-time writer and part-time college instructor in Dallas, Texas (USA). Joli has written several books on Windows operating systems and Adobe software products, and is currently working on her seventh book, *Photoshop 7.0 for Screen Printers and Graphic Aritists*. Joli also writes for Microsoft as an XP Expert Zone columnist, teaches Frontpage and Windows 2000 classes at the local community college, and creates artwork and maintains the computers for North Texas Graphics, a screen printing and embroidery company she co-founded 7 years ago.

Before becoming a professional writer, Joli held such positions as High School Algebra Teacher, Maintenance PC Technician, Network Administrator, and Web Designer. She can be contacted atb *cosmo@waymark.net*.

Introducing Photoshop

1

What is Photoshop?
Cutting through the jargon
What are pixels?
What is resolution?
What are paths?
And never the twain shall meet?
Exploring the interface
Using the Toolbox
Using the Options bar
Using the Menu bar
Using the palettes and the Palette Well
More fun stuff with palettes
Palettes available from the Options bar
Summary

What is Photoshop?

Photoshop 7.0 is a professional image-editing program that allows you to efficiently manipulate images for print, the Web, CDs or any other medium. These images can be photos, logos, hand-drawn art, or a combination of these.

Photoshop 7.0 offers lots of tools for getting the job done right. There are brushes, pens and pencils, lots of selection tools, shape-creation tools, airbrush capabilities, move tools, filters and effects, sharpen and smudge tools, hand and zoom tools and, of course, eraser tools, to name just a few.

There are also several enhancements to the last version of Photoshop. The new File Browser lets you search for images using thumbnails. There's a new Healing Brush, used to remove dust, scratches and other blemishes from old photographs. There's the ability to make Web page elements transparent, so the background will show through, and options to optimise the files you'll use on the Web. You can customise your Photoshop workspace by creating a palette layout and then saving that layout for future use, thus allowing you to create a different workspace for different tasks. You can customise any tool, such as a paintbrush or pencil, and save it as a new, custom tool. The new Auto Color command lets you correct colours in images quickly and painlessly, and there's even a multilingual spell checker. Whatever your needs are, Photoshop 7.0 has them covered!

In this book, I shall introduce all of these things, so that you can get a feel for everything Photoshop offers. In this chapter, we'll begin by learning some words and looking at the workspace.

Cutting through the jargon

You need to know the jargon, or the words used in Photoshop 7.0, to understand the interface and this book. Pixels, bitmaps, vectors, resolution and paths are a few of them.

What are pixels?

Pixels are the building blocks of bitmap images (sometimes called raster images), which are generally photos, either scanned or taken digitally. A pixel is a rectangular block of a single colour. It is the basic unit of colour on a monitor. The actual size of the pixel depends on how the resolution is set, so pixels are not defined by their size. If you draw a diagonal line with the Pencil tool, then zoom in on it, you can see the actual pixel shape. You won't see the pixels on horizontal or vertical lines though, because the pixels are rectangular and thus don't show through. An example of this is shown in Figure 1.1.

When you work with photos or other images, you can define how many pixels per inch or how many pixels per centimetre you want the file to have. The more pixels the image has per unit, the better the quality of colour and resolution.

Figure 1.2 shows the options when creating a new file in Photoshop 7.0. The width and height of the image can be set in pixels. Notice that the default resolution is 72 pixels per inch. That means that each square inch of the image you'll create will contain 72 pixels, or small rectangles. Each of these rectangles will hold a single colour, but because there are so many pixels, you won't be able to tell. Additionally, because the coloured rectangles are so small, they'll blend together to make the colours of the photo appear to blend together as well.

Throughout this book, I'll be using a screen resolution of 1024 × 768 pixels, meaning that the screen is 1024 pixels wide and 768 pixels high. You should use this configuration too. If you can only set a resolution of 800 × 600 pixels, some of the items on your screen won't look the same as in this book.

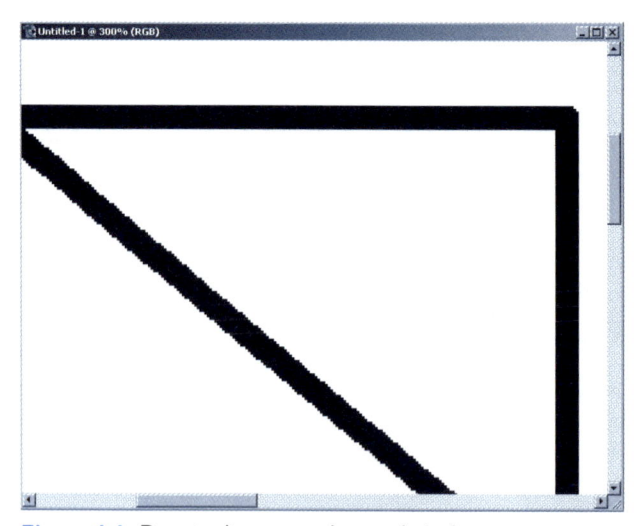

Figure 1.1 Drawing lines to understand pixels.

What is resolution?

Resolution is how many pixels per unit you choose. Pixels and resolution go hand in hand. So how do you decide how many pixels you need per square inch? Well, there are guidelines for this. For general messing around, for viewing the work only on the monitor, and for bitmap images you'll e-mail, 72 pixels per inch is fine. If you want to print the image to a laser or inkjet printer and you'd like a nice output, it is better to choose 200 pixels per inch. If you are sending the artwork or image out to a professional print shop for business cards, flyers, or something along those lines, best to make it 300 pixels per inch.

The more pixels you set, the larger the file will be. If you are concerned about hard drive space, getting the file on a floppy disk, or configuring an image for the Web, don't overdo it!

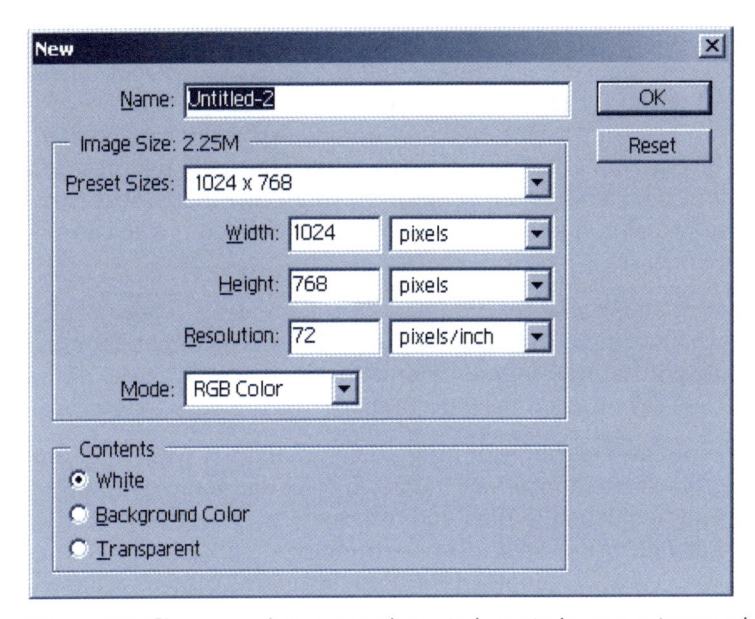

Figure 1.2 Choose resolution in pixels per inch or pixels per centimetre when creating a new file.

What are paths

To understand paths, you first have to understand the nature of a vector image. Vector graphics are considered geometric objects, just like squares, circles and triangles are. They are not bitmap images. A vector image is defined by its corners, radius, location and other similar attributes. For instance, all points on a circle are equidistant from the centre, which is what makes it a circle. All corners of a rectangle are 90 degrees and the sides are parallel. These images can be resized without distortion because the points on them are created mathematically. When they are resized, the graphic is simply recalculated. (This is not true of bitmap images.) This type of art is especially useful when creating logos that will be used first on something small like a business card, and used later to create a sign for the car park, because resized images do not lose their edges or crispness.

You can create vector images using the Pen tool. While creating, a path is also created that defines the outline of the shape. The path consists of path components, such as anchor points, line segments and curves. Because these paths are not pixel based, they take up less hard drive space and are easy to store.

On a path, anchor points define the beginning and end, and are used to define curves in the shape. These anchor points (sometimes called handles in other graphics programs) can be pushed, pulled and otherwise moved, to change the shape of the path. Paths can be created to outline objects in a picture, to a create a new shape, or to create a simple mask. Path segments can be reshaped, deleted, copied or merged.

Paths are only created when creating your own vector graphics and using the Pen or Shape tools.

Paths can be accessed from the Paths palette, but they're only temporary. If you want to use a path you've created in another project and at a later time, you'll have to save it. You'll learn all about paths and the Pen tool in Chapter 5, *Modifying paths*.

And never the twain shall meet?

Vector graphics and bitmap images are the two types of images you'll work with in Photoshop 7.0. A single file can contain both types. Bitmaps use pixels to define an image, while vectors use mathematical formulas. Bitmaps are usually photographs, and when you edit them, you are editing the pixels. Vector graphics are usually shapes and lines, and when you edit those, you are working with their mathematical representation.

Exploring the interface

The Photoshop interface consists of many elements, including the Toolbox, the Menu bar, the Options bar, the Palette Well, the file itself, and the individual palettes. The interface and elements are shown in Figure 1.3.

To work with Photoshop 7.0 effectively, you must know what tools and options are available and where to find them in the interface. Let's look at that now.

Although it looks like quite a bit of stuff to get through, there's a lot of common commands and tools in the Toolbox, palettes and menus.

Using the Toolbox

The **Toolbox** is located on the left side of the work area, but it can be moved anywhere on the screen by dragging from its title bar. The Toolbox contains multiple tools, each represented by an icon, as you can see from Figure 1.3. If there is a small arrow in the bottom right corner of the icon, there are additional tools available besides the one visible. These are called hidden tools. To see these additional (hidden) tools, click on them and hold down the mouse button for a second. A drop-down list will appear with the names of the tools available.

You can hover the mouse over a tool in the toolbox and a pop-up will appear with its name.

Photoshop 7

The first time you open Photoshop 7.0, you might be prompted to register or to configure colour settings. You can do either if you want — just follow the directions on the screen.

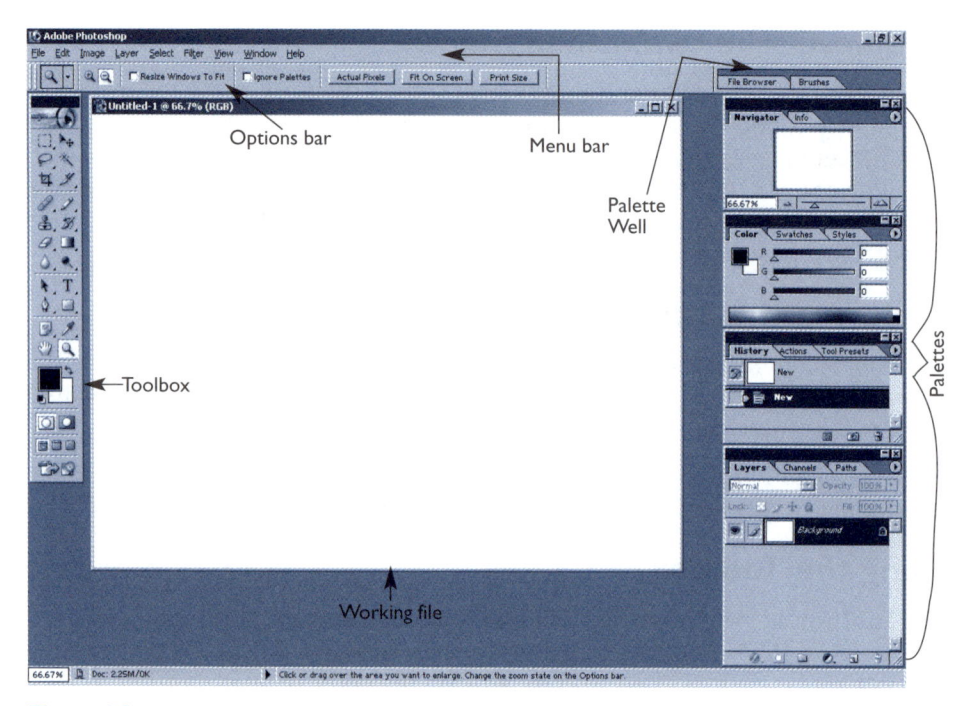

Figure 1.3 Understanding the Photoshop 7.0 interface.

To experiment with the tools in the Toolbox:

1. Open Photoshop 7.0 and locate the Toolbox.
2. Click the mouse on the first tool in the left-hand corner of the Toolbox, the **Marquee** tool, and hold down the mouse for about a second.
3. The four choices that appear are shown in Figure 1.4.
4. To select any of these tools, move the mouse over it and click once. (Notice that the options on the Options bar change each time you select a different tool.)

If you choose the Rectangular Marquee tool, the icon will remain a rectangle, as shown in Figure 1.3. If the Elliptical Marquee tool is chosen, the icon will change to an ellipse. If the Single Row or Single Column Marquee tools are chosen, the icon changes again. The icon changes each time a tool is chosen to

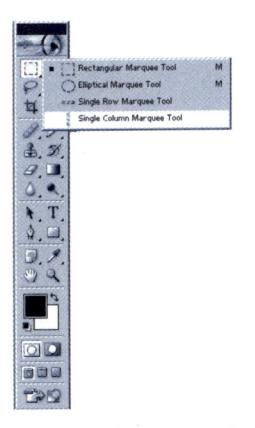

Figure 1.4 Locating the Marquee tool in the Toolbox.

Photoshop 7

Click once quickly on any icon to use the tool that's showing. To select a different tool from the hidden options, click once and hold down the mouse button for about a second. Then, choose the tool you want to use from the list.

reflect that change, and to show the icon of the tool that's in use. Throughout this book, therefore, your Toolbox may look different from the ones in the screenshots, depending on what you have chosen as the default tools.

The same is true of the other tools. Figure 1.5 shows the Toolbox with the default tool that you'll see when you first open the program.

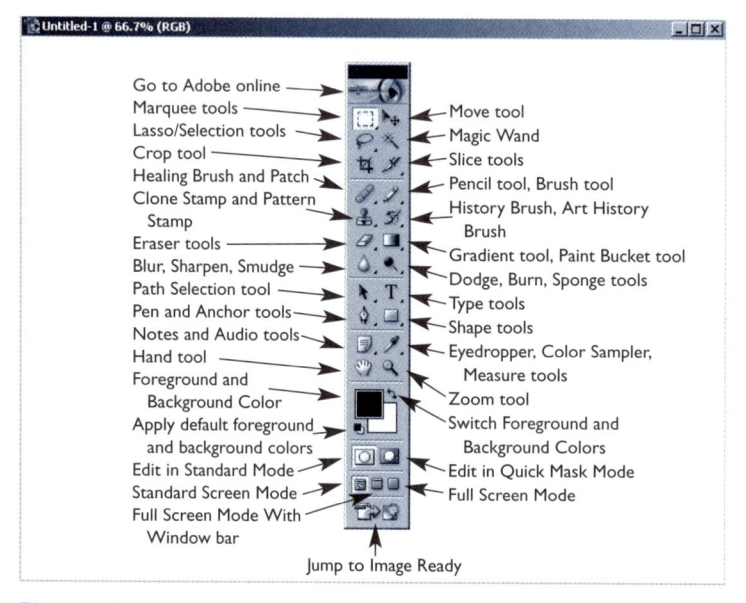

```
Go to Adobe online
Marquee tools ─────────→       ←─── Move tool
Lasso/Selection tools ────→    ←─── Magic Wand
Crop tool ────────────────→    ←─── Slice tools
Healing Brush and Patch ──→    ←─── Pencil tool, Brush tool
Clone Stamp and Pattern         ←─── History Brush, Art History
  Stamp                               Brush
Eraser tools ─────────────→
Blur, Sharpen, Smudge ────→    ←─── Gradient tool, Paint Bucket tool
Path Selection tool ──────→    ←─── Dodge, Burn, Sponge tools
Pen and Anchor tools ─────→    ←─── Type tools
Notes and Audio tools ────→    ←─── Shape tools
Hand tool ────────────────→    ←─── Eyedropper, Color Sampler,
Foreground and                        Measure tools
  Background Color                ←─── Zoom tool
Apply default foreground         ←─── Switch Foreground and
  and background colors                Background Colors
Edit in Standard Mode ────→    ←─── Edit in Quick Mask Mode
Standard Screen Mode ─────→    ←─── Full Screen Mode
Full Screen Mode With
  Window bar
              Jump to Image Ready
```

Figure 1.5 The tools are located in the Toolbox and have specific default settings.

The object of this book is to teach you how to use all of these tools. Of course, you aren't expected to know what they all do right now! As these tools are introduced throughout the book, refer back to Figure 1.5 as necessary.

Using the Options bar

The **Options bar** also changes frequently. In fact, each time a tool is chosen from the Toolbox, the Options bar is transformed. Did you notice when you selected the Rectangular Marquee tool that the options on the Option bar suddenly offered all kinds of options for configuring rectangles?

Let's experiment by selecting some tools and watching the Options bar change:

1. Click on the **Rectangular Marquee** tool again, and look at the Options bar. (It's the grey bar underneath the menu bar at the top of the screen.) You can set options for how you want the rectangle to look. We'll explore these options in later chapters.
2. Click on the **Eraser** tool and look at the Options bar. Now you can set brush size and opacity as well as other options. You'll become quite familiar with the erasers!
3. Click on the **Type** tool. Notice that you can now set font, colour, size, style, justification, and more. More about adding type in Chapter 8.

The idea behind this is simple: you choose a tool, and then make configuration changes from the Options bar. Depending on the tool, you can set colour, size of the stroke, hardness, opacity, and lots more.

As you make changes to the Options bar, the default settings change. Because of this, your Options bar may not always look like the Options bar in the screenshots in this book. You can reset the Options bar to its defaults by right-

*With several of the tools, the options in the Options bar not only offer a place to make configuration changes, like for the Type tool, but can also offer palettes for choosing between multiple available tools. The Eraser tool offers such a palette. Click on the down arrow next to **Brush** to see the palette and brush options.*

It's a good idea to reset the tools often when first learning Photoshop. This way, you become familiar with the defaults, and your screen will look more like the ones you see in this book.

clicking once on the icon farthest to the left on the Options bar. You'll then have two choices: Reset Tool or Reset All Tools. Choose **Reset Tool** to return all of the options in the Options bar to its default. Choose **Reset All Tools** to reset all Options bars to their defaults.

Using the Menu bar

Using the **Menu bar** is easy. In fact, it's just like using any other menu bar in any other program. Just click on a menu, and look at the options in the drop-down list. Select the option you want, and you're ready to work.

Take a look at all of the menu choices so you can familiarise yourself with where everything is located:

1. Click once on the **File** menu. From the drop-down list, notice that this menu is similar to other file menus you've used. You can choose from New, Open, Close, Save, Print, Import, Export, and other familiar options. In this book I'll denote choosing one of these options like this: **File > Open**, **File > Print**, **File > Save As**.

2. On the **Edit** menu, you'll see tools that are used for editing. Step Backward undoes the last operation you did, for instance, and there are several others. From this menu, you can choose **Edit > Preferences > General** to personalise your workspace. For now, however, let's stick with the defaults and refrain from personalising just yet. This way, our screens will look the same.

3. Open the remaining menus and look at the options. You'll see there's some redundancy, for instance the **View > Zoom In** option is also available from the Toolbox by clicking on the Zoom tool.

Using the palettes and the Palette Well

Palettes are those boxes you see on the right of your screen (see Figure 1.6). The default palettes are the Navigator palette, Color palette, History palette and Layers palette. Palettes help you view the attributes of an image and to edit it. Like the other interface features, they can be dragged to other areas of the screen. You'll use the palettes often when working.

Let's take a look at the default palettes for a computer with display settings of 1024 × 768:

1. Open a new file by selecting **File > New**.
2. In the **New** dialogue box that appears, type in the word *'Palette Test'* for the file name.
3. Choose 800 × 600, a white background, 72 ppi and RGB colour. Press **OK**.
4. Choose **Window > Workspace > Reset Palette Locations** to make sure you have the defaults. If you look at the **Layers palette**, you will see that there is only one layer and it is named Background – unlike Figure 1.6, which has two.
5. Click on the **Type** tool in the toolbox (it's the eighth one down the right side), then click anywhere in the new file. Type the word *'Test'*. Notice now that a new layer has been created in the Layers palette, named Layer 1. (Layers are viewed under the Layers tab.)
6. Type the word *'Test'* on to the page.
7. Click inside the layer box on the layer named Layer 1. Notice that the name of the layer changes to Test. You can see this in Figure 1.6. As you add images, text and other objects, new layers can be (and often are automatically) added.

14 Photoshop 7

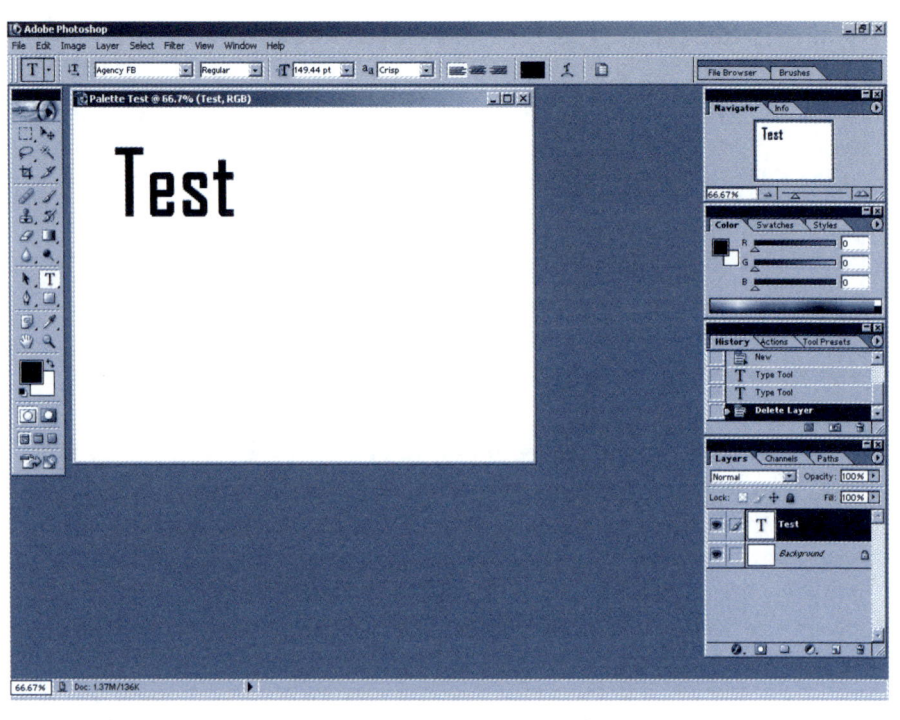

Figure 1.6 Use the default palettes to view the attributes of an image and edit it.

You can then edit the layers independently of one another, without disrupting the other text, images and objects in other layers of the image. Layers are covered in depth in Chapter 6.

8. Look at the **History palette**. Here, you can go back through your operations, undoing steps you've already done. Click on the line that contains the word New. The text you added disappears, because you've 'undone' everything you did after the New command.

9. Look at the **Navigator palette**. This palette helps you keep track of your file and its progress, and lets you view the image in different ways using the Hand tool. Because the Hand tool is available from the Toolbox, you might not use this palette too much – you can remove it later if you decide you don't need it.

10. The **Color palette** is the second palette. The Color palette displays the current value of the foreground and background colours. Use the sliders in this palette to edit these colours. There are several colour models to choose from. Click on the other tabs in the Color palette to view these. Colours will be detailed in Chapters 2 and 4.

11. Finally, notice that each palette has a right arrow in its top right corner. Clicking this arrow brings up the following additional options:

    - The **Navigator** palette offers Palette Options, which allows you to change the colour of the viewing area. Red is the default. You can also dock the palette to the Palette Well (discussed shortly).

    - The **Color** palette offers different options for each of its three tabs. For the Color tab, there are options for choosing different colour schemes and colour spectrums. The default is RGB (red, green and blue), but you

The History tab also has a slider that you can use to select the place to revert to. This is typical of many of the tools and options. Many contain places to click, places to type in a specific number or level, or a slider to move to a specific point. When these additional options exist, you can use whatever option you prefer; all do the same thing in the end.

can change to CMYK (cyan, magenta, yellow and black), Greyscale, and others. For the Swatches tab, you can change from the default colours to Pantone, Mac, Web-safe colour schemes, and more, as well as change the view of the palette itself. In the Styles tab, the options include changing the views and the types of styles shown.

- The **Layers** palette also offers additional options for each of its tabs. With the Layers tab chosen, you can add or delete a layer, duplicate and flatten layers, and more. The other tabs, Channels and Paths, offer additional options, which will be covered later.
- The **History** palette offers options to Step Backward, Step Forward, Clear History and create a new document, among other things. Stepping backward is undoing, while stepping forward is undoing what has just been undone. You can also set tool presets, and set and define actions.

Now that you've played around with the default palettes, let's look at some of the other palette options.

You can move the palettes if you want. To move a palette to another area of the screen, drag it using its title bar (the blue bar at the top of the palette). Just click and hold on the title bar then drag it across the screen with the mouse. Figure 1.7 shows the default palettes after they have been moved.

You can also make the palettes larger or smaller by clicking and holding on their corners and dragging inwards or outwards with the mouse. In Figure 1.7, the Layers palette and the Navigator palette have been enlarged in this manner.

1: Introducing Photoshop 17

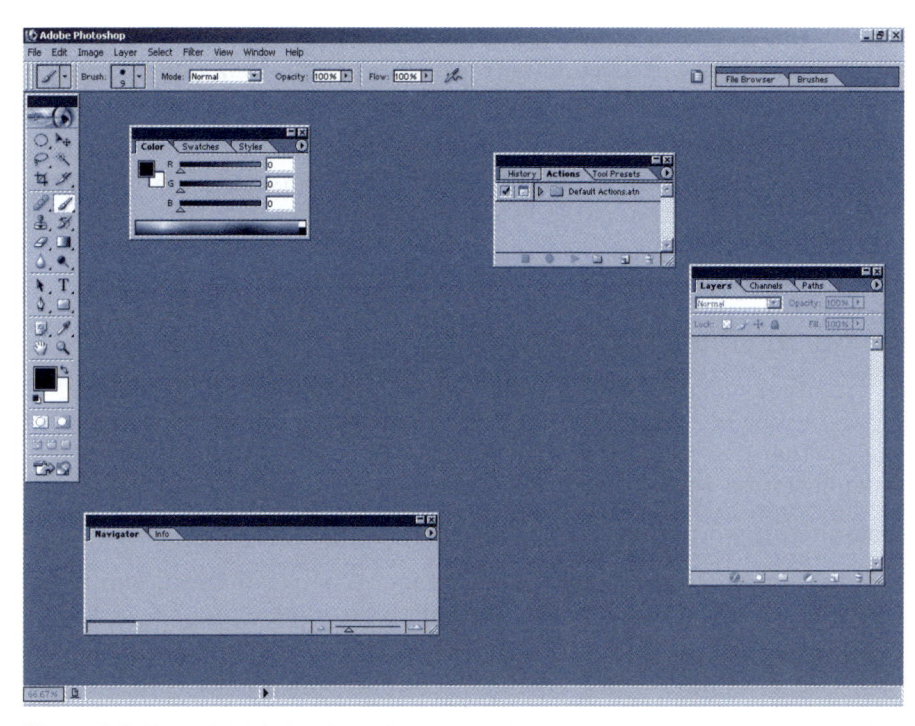

Figure 1.7 Move the default palettes by dragging them, or resize the palettes by pulling from the corners.

You can also choose Window menu options to hide or show the Status bar, Options bar and Toolbox.

Finally, you can use the **Window** menu to show or hide any of the palettes, by placing or removing the checkmark in front of the palette desired. For instance, removing the checkmark from the **Window > Color** option removes the Color palette from the work area; conversely, rechecking it again puts it back.

After resetting, resizing, and hiding or showing the tools and palettes, return them to their default states using **Window > Workspace > Reset Palette Locations**. This also returns the Options bar, Status bar and other palettes to their original location.

More fun stuff with palettes

There are other ways to use and edit palettes besides moving, resizing or hiding them. For instance, you can dock palettes together or dock parts of palettes to other palettes, and you can also use the Palette Well to manage and dock open palettes.

Let's move the History tab of the Layers palette to the Navigator palette:

1. Move the palettes around so there's space in between them, similar to Figure 1.7. (This will make moving the palettes easier.)
2. Click on the **History** tab of the **History** palette, and hold down the left mouse button while dragging this tab to the **Navigator** palette. Release the mouse once there. The History tab will now be docked with the Navigator palette and will no longer be in the History palette.
3. Do the same with the **Actions** tab. Once finished, reset the palettes with **Window > Workspace > Reset Palette Locations**.

You can dock palettes on the Options bar too. This is quite handy when you need more workspace because it removes the palette from the screen, but still allows it to be available easily from the Options bar. To dock a palette on to the Options bar:

1. Make sure your display is set to something larger than 800 × 600, or else you won't be able to dock to the Options bar. 1024 × 768 is recommended: you'll have to make the change through the display properties of your computer.
2. Drag a tab of a palette to the right-hand corner of the Options bar and then let go of it. This is called the Palette Well. In Figure 1.8, you can see the Palette Well, with some of the missing palettes docked there.

Here are some additional tips and tricks when working with palettes:

- Use the **Tab** key to switch between showing no palettes, no option bar and no toolbox, to showing all of them. Just open a new file, hit the **Tab** key, and see what happens!
- Drag a single tab from a palette to the work area to create a palette for that tab only.
- Click on the X to close a palette or click on the dash to minimize it.
- Click the right arrow, available in many places and palettes, to see the pop-up menu, which contains additional options for that tool.

To move an entire palette, such as the Navigator palette, simply drag all of the tabs over. Once moved, the palette (or tab) will no longer appear in the work area; it will be docked in the Palette Well.

Figure 1.8 Moving palettes and tabs to the Palette Well.

- Pull a palette from the Palette Well to the work area if you want it to remain on the work area. Otherwise, simply click on it in the Palette Well to work with it once. After the selection has been made and the task finished, the palette will disappear back to the Palette Well when the next tool is chosen.
- The configuration of the palettes and other tools are saved when you exit the program. This means, that the next time you open the program the last workspace configuration will be used. To always start with the default palette locations, choose **Edit > Preferences > General**, deselect **Save Palette Locations** and click **OK**.
- If you get the palettes set just the way you want them, you can save the configuration using the **Window > Workspace > Save Workspace** option. Just type in a name for the workspace, such as '*Painting*' or '*Photo Editing*', and click **Save**.

Palettes available from the Options bar

Believe it or not, there are even more palettes! These palettes are available from the Options bar when specific tools are chosen from the Toolbox. You'll get palettes when choosing tools such as the Brush and Pencil tools, the Healing Brush tool, the Patch tool, the Clone Stamp and Pattern Stamp tools, the History Brush and Artbrush tools, all of the Eraser tools, the Gradient tool, the Blur, Sharpen and Smudge tools, the Dodge, Burn and Sponge tools, and all of the Shape tools.

These palettes are a little different from the palettes detailed earlier in this chapter, as they can't be moved, dragged or docked to the Palette Well like other palettes can. Their purpose is to offer you additional choices for a tool, like a brush. For instance, when choosing the Brush tool from the Toolbox, the Options bar changes to offer a palette that contains brush types. There are lots of brushes to choose from.

Let's look at some palettes from the Options bar:

1. Open a new file by selecting **File > New**. Configure the new file's options as the default, or experiment with other options.
2. Click on the **Brush** tool (fourth tool on the right in the Toolbox) and hold down the mouse button for a second to see the menu choices. Choose **Brush Tool**.
3. Locate the **Brush** options on the Options bar.
4. Click the down arrow next to **Brush**. You'll see several different brushes to choose from. See Figure 1.9.
5. In this Brush palette, there is a right arrow. Click on this right arrow to see additional options. This is also shown in Figure 1.9.
6. In Figure 1.9, **Stroke Thumbnail** is ticked. You can select any other viewing option you want, though; I prefer **Large List**. Large List allows me to see the name and a small thumbnail of the brush.
7. From the list on the right, choose **Assorted Brushes**, and then click **OK** to verify the change. New, assorted brushes will be loaded into the Brush palette.
8. Select the other types of brushes too; the **Faux Finish** brushes are nice. When finished, choose **Reset Brushes**, and click **OK** to return to the default brushes.

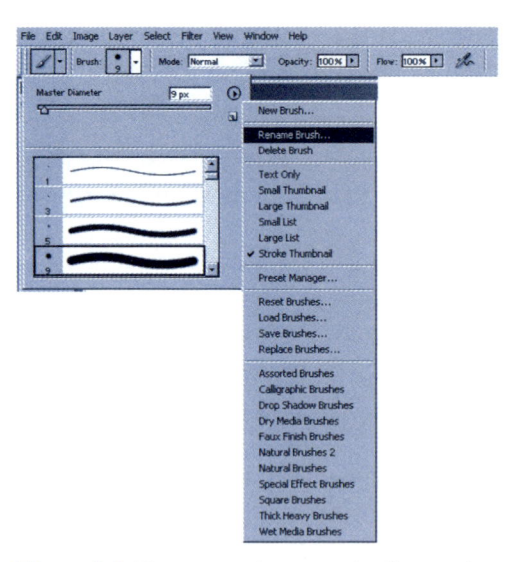

Figure 1.9 There are palettes on the Options bar too.

You can see other palettes by selecting other tools from the Toolbox and then clicking on the appropriate down arrows in the Options bar. Throughout this book, you'll learn about many of the options.

Summary

In this chapter you learned about pixels, resolution, paths, and vector and bitmap images. You also learned how to navigate through the Photoshop 7.0 interface, including how to use the Toolbox, Options bar and palettes.

Enhancing photos   2

Opening a photo
Using the Open command
Using the File Browser
Acquiring an image from your scanner
Connecting a digital camera to your PC
Choosing the right view
Using the Zoom tool
Using the Hand tool
Display size, image size and file size
Adjusting the picture information
Making automatic adjustments
Working with brightness and contrast
Changing the hue and saturation
Tweaking the colour levels
Creating instant photonegatives
Minding the History palette
Saving your work
Summary

So, you've taken some pictures, and you are ready to enhance them with Photoshop 7.0. Hopefully you had the opportunity to take the photos with a digital camera, but pictures taken with a disposable or regular film camera can be used as well. In this chapter, you'll learn how to get those photos on to your computer, either by downloading them from your digital camera or by scanning them in. Once the picture is in the computer, you can let Photoshop adjust the pictures automatically, or you can change the brightness, contrast, saturation or hue yourself. You can also create photonegatives, zoom in on a photo, and tweak the colour levels.

Opening a photo

There are only a few ways to open a photo you want to edit. If you already have it in your computer you can open it using **File > Open**; you can acquire it from your digital camera by downloading the image and saving it to the hard drive; or you scan an existing, physical photograph using a scanner. You can also use a new feature, the File Browser. Let's start with the easiest, and use the **Open** command.

Using the Open command

Figure 2.1 shows the Open dialogue box. Yours probably looks different from this, due to several factors. This is what the dialogue box looks like on a PC, and the Look In window shows Samples. Your Look In window will show the last place in which you opened a file in Photoshop 7.0, and may be different.

To open a file already on your computer, you can browse to it using this dialogue box. The Look In window has a down arrow beside it; click it and locate the folder your files are saved in. For practice, let's open a file from the Samples folder in Photoshop 7.0.

2: Enhancing photos

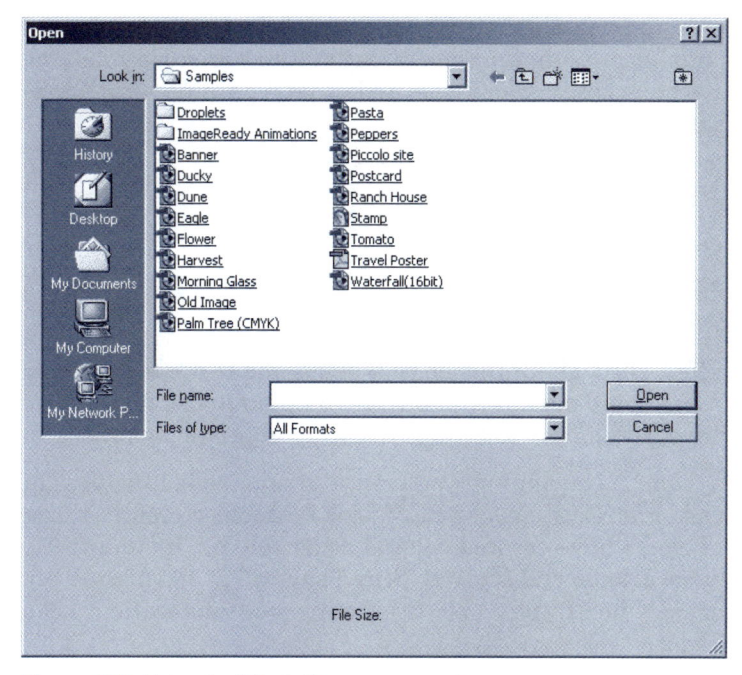

[Figure: Open dialog box screenshot showing Samples folder with files including Droplets, ImageReady Animations, Banner, Ducky, Dune, Eagle, Flower, Harvest, Morning Glass, Old Image, Palm Tree (CMYK), Pasta, Peppers, Piccolo site, Postcard, Ranch House, Stamp, Tomato, Travel Poster, Waterfall(16bit)]

Figure 2.1 Using the **File > Open** command.

1. Open the Open dialogue box using **File > Open** (Figure 2.1). (If the Samples folder is showing, work through these steps anyway, just for practice.)
2. Click the down arrow by the Look In window.

3. Choose your root drive from the list. Generally, this is denoted as **Local Disk (C:)**. If you dual boot with other operating systems or store your program files on another disk, choose the disk that contains the Adobe Photoshop program files.
4. From the new choices, choose **Program Files**.
5. From the new choices, choose **Adobe**.
6. From the new choices, chose **Photoshop 7.0**.
7. From the new choices, choose **Samples**.
8. From the choices, choose **Peppers**.

You've just opened a file! Throughout this book, when asked to open a file from the Samples folder, you should open it this way. If you plan to use files you've saved to your hard drive, you'll have to browse to the appropriate folder.

Let me suggest that, from the beginning, you create a folder called Pictures or use the My Pictures folder already on your PC. Inside that folder, create others. In my My Pictures folder, I have created several other folders, including My Videos, My Kids, My Vacations, and My Web Site. I save all of the pictures in the appropriate folder, so when I want a picture from my latest vacation, I can go to that folder to find it.

Using the File Browser

Another feature of Photoshop 7.0 is the **File Browser**. This is one of the greatest features ever created. It wasn't in earlier versions of Photoshop either, so it's brand new. The File Browser lets you look at all of the files on your computer using thumbnails. Figure 2.2 shows an example.

2: Enhancing photos

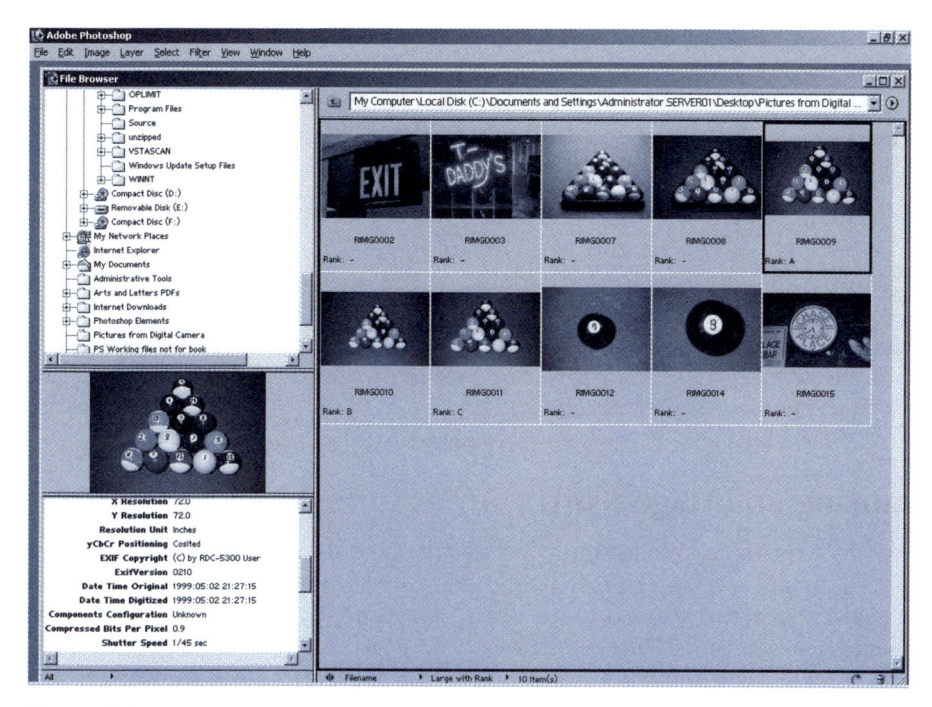

Figure 2.2 Use the File Browser to browse all of the files on your computer.

Use the File Browser to browse your computer for image files, view thumbnails of images before selecting them, and view an image's attributes. Right-click on any photo to open it, delete it, rotate it or view its location. This is an extremely useful addition to the programme that makes searching for and finding files

The first time you use the File Browser, it might not fit properly on your screen. Use the **Tab** *key to remove everything from the workspace except for the active item, which can either be the image itself or the File Browser. The* **Tab** *key puts Photoshop in Full Screen Mode, and thus removes the Toolbox, all of the palettes and the menu bar.*

WIA Support is only available if you are using Windows ME or Windows XP.

much easier. You can browse to anywhere on your computer's hard drive, CD drive or floppy drive, and even to some types of digital cameras. After choosing a photo from the File Browser, a preview of the image is shown in the left pane, and the file's attributes are listed. Attributes listed include file name, date created, date modified, image format, file size and colour mode, and lots more.

When using the File Browser for the first time, you'll notice that it is attached to the Palette Well. Working with palettes from the Palette Well can be trying, because after you move on to another step or choose another tool, it disappears back in to the Well. If this is what you want, that's fine. I usually prefer to drag it from the Palette Well to the work area, and then hit the **Tab** key to have enough space for viewing. Figure 2.2 shows the File Browser standing on its own. (To drag it from the Palette Well, grab it by its tab and pull while holding down the mouse button.) This way, it stays on the screen until I'm ready to close it.

Acquiring an image from your scanner

In order to acquire an image from your scanner, you'll need to have the scanner connected up and working properly. You'll also need to install it using the directions that came with your scanner. With that done, you can acquire pictures from your scanner using **File > Import**.

To acquire an image from your scanner, first try **File > Import** and choose the scanner from the list, and if that doesn't work try **File > Import > WIA Support**. You'll be able to follow the directions from there to obtain the image from the scanner. Depending on the scanner, driver and operating system you are using, this might or might not work. If you can't scan an Image from inside Photoshop 7.0, use the scanner's own software to scan the image, save the file to the to the hard drive as a TIFF file, then open the file in Photoshop by browsing to it.

Connecting a digital camera to you PC

The best way to go about connecting that new digital camera to your PC is to follow the instructions that came with it. There are many different types of digital cameras, so the methods used to transfer the photos from them to your computer can differ greatly. For many digital cameras you must first turn off the camera before you connect the power supply and USB cable to the camera, then connect the power supply to the wall outlet and USB cable to the computer, and finally turn the camera back on.

Some cameras don't have to be connected at all, and instead save pictures to a floppy disk or memory card that is removed from the camera and inserted into a separate physical device connected to the computer. Sometimes this is the floppy drive (A:), and sometimes it is a separate memory card reader.

After the camera, floppy or memory card is connected or inserted, it will act just like a drive with data on it. If it's a floppy disk, you'll get the files from the A: drive. If it's a separate card reader, perhaps the E: or F: drives. If the camera must be physically connected to the computer to download the pictures, you might have two drives (one for the camera and one for an additional memory card inside the camera). Because it is seen by the computer as a drive, you can browse to the pictures using the File Browser or by choosing **File > Open**.

I'm assuming that you've already installed the camera, the device drivers and the software that came with the camera. If you haven't done that yet, do it now.

Photoshop 7

*If the camera connects directly to the computer, don't just turn off the camera when you are finished with it. Not all cameras are designed to work this way. Look for the **Eject** or **Unplug Hardware** option on your taskbar, double-click on it and stop the device before physically turning it off or removing it from your system.*

You can also obtain images from the camera in the same manner you obtained them from the scanner, using **File > Import**. Just select your camera from the list, and follow the directions that appear. As with scanners, this may or may not work, depending on the camera, the drivers and the operating system you are using. It's usually easier to work with the camera as detailed next.

Let's practice getting a picture from a digital camera:

1. Connect the camera to the PC using its USB, serial or other type of cable, or remove the floppy disk or card from the camera and insert it into the PC.
2. If connecting the camera physically, turn on the camera and set it to its PC setting.
3. Choose **File > Browse**.
4. From the top-left window of the File Browser box, scroll down to the drive that contains the pictures and click on it.
5. If necessary, open any other folders that contain photos. (Sometimes this occurs because there is a card in the camera.)
6. Use the File Browser to locate the image you want, and double-click on it to open it. (You can also right-click and choose **Open**.)

Choosing the right view

Choosing how to view your image (once it's open) depends solely on what you want to do with it. If you need to trace around an object, for instance, you'll want to zoom in on it to see the details of the outline. If you want to see an entire image that is too big for your screen, you'll want to zoom out. You can view your image in almost any magnification level you want, and these levels are defined by percentages. For instance, you can zoom out to 0.29% and in to 1600% of the image's original size. When zooming, this percentage of magnification is shown in the title bar.

After you've zoomed in, you won't be able to see the entire image. This is when the Hand tool is useful. The Hand tool allows you to move the image around on the screen, without having to use the scroll bars. In the following sections, you'll learn how to use the Zoom and Hand tools to effectively manipulate and edit your images.

Using the Zoom tool

When you use the **Zoom** tool, you aren't changing the actual size or dimensions of the image; you're just changing just how you view it. There are several ways to zoom in on an image using the View menu:

- **View > Zoom In** enlarges the display of the image by a percentage. Use the tool repeatedly to enlarge it even more. The percentage the image is enlarged from the original can be seen from the title bar. The Navigator palette places a rectangle around the part of the image that has been zoomed in on. Figure 2.3 shows an example.
- **View > Zoom Out** reduces the display of the image. Use the tool repeatedly to reduce the image even more. The Navigator palette and the Title bar offer information about the zoom process.
- **View > Fit On Screen** resizes the image so that it fits in your work area optimally.

*You can also open an image from the **File > Open** command. Just browse to the location of the images and select one to open. Refer to the section **Using the open command** if you need help.*

*Once you've selected an image using the File Browser, double-click on the image to open it or right-click and choose **Open**; if you've browsed to it using **File > Open**, just click on it once from the list of images in the Open window.*

Figure 2.3 Use **View > Zoom In** to enlarge an image. The Navigator palette and the Title bar offer information about the zoom process.

Besides the menu options, the Zoom tool from the Toolbox can also be used. The Zoom tool is the eleventh tool down the right side of the Toolbox, and looks like a magnifying glass. When this tool is chosen, the cursor changes to a magnifying glass with a plus sign in it. Using this new cursor, you can click on the image wherever you want to zoom in or out on it. This tool can also be used to select a portion of the image to zoom. These are not options when using the **View > Zoom** commands, and makes the Zoom tool more effective.

To use the Zoom tool from the Toolbox:

1. Open an image or file. If you don't have any, open any image from the Sample folder as shown earlier in this chapter.
2. Click on the **Zoom** tool – the cursor changes to a magnifying glass. Use the mouse to position the cursor over part of the image and click once. Notice that the image is zoomed in on.
3. Right-click on the image and choose **Zoom Out** to return the image to its original view. (This might have to be done several times.)
4. This time click and drag the mouse across a part of the image. This produces a rectangle and allows you to select only a specific part of the image. When you stop dragging the mouse and let go of it, the selection will be zoomed in on.
5. This time, hold down either the **Alt** key (on a PC) or the **Option** key (on a Mac) when clicking with the Zoom tool. This enables you to zoom out instead of in. (You won't be able to select a part of the image to zoom out on, however.)
6. Double-click on the Zoom tool in the Toolbox to return quickly to 100% view.
7. Now choose the **Move** tool. It's the first tool in the Toolbox on the right side. Now, on the keyboard, select **Shift+Z** (on a PC) or **Option+Z** (on a Mac) to

Hold down the Ctrl key and the plus sign to zoom in, or the Ctrl key and the minus sign to zoom out.

When using files from the Samples folder, don't save any changes you've made or you'll write over the original Samples file. If you want to save the image, rename it first. See Saving your work later in this chapter.

You can use the scroll bars on the right and bottom sides of the image to perform the same tasks as using the Hand tool. However, using the Hand tool is generally more efficient.

quickly return to the Zoom tool. This is a good shortcut to know, because the zoom tools are used quite often while editing.

8. Finally, use the **View > Zoom In**, **View > Zoom Out**, and **View > Fit on Screen** to zoom in and out on the image.

While using the Zoom tool, you won't be able to see the entire image. This is where the Hand tool comes into play.

Using the Hand tool

You'll only need the **Hand** tool when the image is too large for the viewing window. If you try to use it otherwise, it won't do anything.

Follow these steps to learn how to use the Hand tool:

1. Open any image. If you don't have an image of you own yet, open an image from the Samples folder as shown earlier in this chapter. (Flower.psd is a nice picture.)
2. Click on the **Move** tool (it's the first tool in the Toolbox on the right side).
3. Click and hold the cursor on the bottom right corner of the image and push inward, until only about half of your image is showing.
4. Click on the **Hand** tool in the Toolbox. It's the eleventh one down the left side and is next to the Zoom tool.
5. Place the hand in the image window, click and drag. As you move the mouse, the image area will change.
6. Select the **Move** tool again.
7. Using the keyboard, hold down the **Spacebar** and the left mouse button to use the Hand tool again.

Display size, image size and file size

Before we get too much further into images and viewing and so on, let's make sure you know the differences between display size, image size and file size. The Zoom and Hand tools change how an image is displayed on the screen, and thus affect only the display size. Image size is different.

Image size is the actual physical size of the image. Image sizes are determined by pixel dimensions, print dimensions and the resolution of an image. You'll get different image sizes by scanning and when using different types of digital cameras. When zooming, you aren't changing the image size; to do that you'll have to use **Image > Image Size**. Changing the image size changes how large it appears on the screen, and how large it will print out on paper.

When resizing images, use the Resize Image Wizard to walk you through the process. Click **Help** *>* **Resize Image** *and follow the on-screen instructions.*

File size is neither display size nor image size. File size is measured in kilobytes (KB), megabytes (MB) and gigabytes (GB). File size is determined by how much hard drive space it takes to store the image. This becomes an important factor when working with a computer with limited hard drive space. File size is also the main concern of Web designers, since the larger the file is, the longer it will take for the user to download the image to their computer. Generally, reducing the image size reduces the file size. In addition, saving in various file formats can decrease file size. For more on file formats and file sizes, refer to Chapter 10.

Adjusting the picture information

Now that you've opened an image, learned how to zoom in and out, and understand the scroll bars and the Hand tool, it's time to start adjusting the image. This is generally referred to as optimising the image, and Photoshop offers lots of ways to do that. You can make automatic adjustments to brightness and contrast, to colours, and more. In this section, you'll learn about these automatic adjustments to images and also about some manual ones.

Making automatic adjustments

The creators of Photoshop 7.0 want you to get the best images possible from your digital camera or scanner. Because of this, they've included several automatic adjustments that enable you to optimise your photos quickly and easily. The following options are some of the few available from the **Image** menu:

- **Image > Adjustments > Auto Contrast**;
- **Image > Adjustments > Auto Colors**;
- **Image > Adjustments > Color Balance**;
- **Image > Adjustments > Brightness/Contrast**;
- **Image > Adjustments > Hue/Saturation**;
- **Image > Adjustments > Desaturate**;
- **Image > Adjustments > Variations**.

These are quite powerful tools for adjusting and optimising images, and I shall describe each of them in the next few sections.

Working with brightness and contrast

Understanding how brightness affects an image is easy; it's how bright or dull a picture is. Perhaps the flash didn't go off as planned, your subject was standing under a shady tree, or the sunlight was too bright, thus making the photo too light or too dark. You can adjust the brightness of a photo simply by adding or removing light.

Contrast, on the other hand, is how the dark and light parts of the image relate. When all of the objects in the image are similar in colour and lighting, such as a picture of a statue or the beach, the contrast might need a little tweaking. When adding contrast, you are telling the computer to make the dark pixels darker and the light pixels lighter, so that there is a better distinction between the objects. Lowering contrast does just the opposite by bringing the colours and shades closer together.

The **Image > Adjustments > Brightness/Contrast** and **Image > Adjustments > Auto Contrast** commands are available to help you solve problems related to brightness and contrast. Follow these steps to learn how to use these commands:

1. Open any image you have on your hard drive. Don't open one from the Samples folder, because some of the options might be greyed out. With your own image, all of the options will be available.

2. Choose **Image > Adjustments > Auto Contrast**. You'll see an hourglass where the cursor used to be, indicating that Photoshop is performing a task. If the Auto Contrast automatic adjustment suits your needs, you're finished with this part of the editing; if not, choose **Edit > Undo Auto Contrast** to remove it.

3. To manually adjust brightness and contrast, choose **Image > Adjustments > Brightness/Contrast** to open the **Brightness/Contrast** dialogue box. Drag the dialogue box to a free area of the workspace so that it does not cover up the image you are working on.

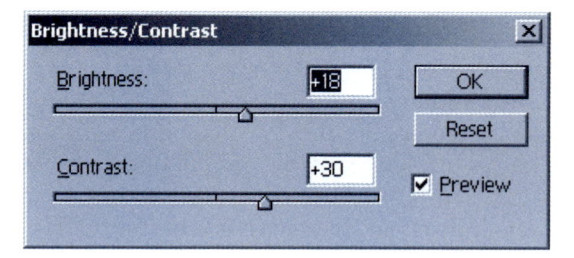

Figure 2.4 Use the Brightness/Contrast dialogue box to enhance an image.

4. From the Brightness/Contrast dialogue box, move the slider for the brightness and the slider for the contrast to enhance the image. Make sure that there's a tick in the **Preview** box. You'll see the changes made to the image as you move the sliders. See Figure 2.4.

Because images, photos and other artwork all contain differing amounts of colours, blacks, whites, midtones, shadows, casts and other attributes, there are no hard and fast rules for configuring these settings. For the most part, it's just personal preference. Trust your instincts, and adjust the settings as you see fit. Later, as you get more experience with Photoshop, try using the **Image > Histogram** command and compare the attributes of what you consider a 'good' image with what you consider a 'bad' one. The Histogram tells you how these different colours and tones are separated and defined, and can be quite useful. For now, let's just concentrate on making the photograph or image look the way we want it to.

Changing the hue and saturation

Two other types of adjustments are available – hue and saturation. Hue and saturation, along with lightness (similar to brightness or brilliance), can be set from the **Image > Adjustments > Hue/Saturation** command. So just what are hue and saturation?

Hue, for our purposes, is basically just a colour, such as red, green or blue. When the hue is off in an image, the colours aren't correct (for instance, an Exit sign looks orange instead of red). Hue can be changed to correct colours in an image.

Saturation is how pure the colour is. As saturation increases, colours seem more pure, or richer. As saturation decreases, colours appear faded or washed out, and look dull.

To practise adjusting the hue and saturation, follow this example:

1. Open the Peppers.jpg image in the Samples folder.
2. Choose **Image > Adjustments > Hue/Saturation** to open the **Hue/Saturation** dialogue box. Drag the dialogue box to an area of the workspace so that it doesn't cover up the image.
3. First make sure that **Preview** is ticked, then move the slider for the hue to +22. Notice that the red peppers now look orange and yellow. By increasing the hue, you are changing the colours.
4. Move the **Hue** slider to –124 to make everything blue. Move the slider back to zero.
5. Move the **Saturation** slider to –44 – notice how greys are added to the picture and the colour appears washed out.

Open one of your own images that's off in colour. Practise using the hue sliders to change the colours so they look better.

6. Move the **Saturation** slider to +21 – notice how the colours become brighter and truer. As you can tell, though, too much saturation is not good. The colours become too bright and look off. Return the **Saturation** slider to 0.
7. Move the **Lightness** slider to the left and right to add or subtract whites and blacks to the image. Click **Cancel** to return to the work area.

While hue and saturation can be set to correct colour, they can also be used to add effect to an image. For instance, you can change the colour of the sky in a photograph from light blue to purple, or change the colour of a pool ball or croquet ball.

You can totally desaturate an image easily too. Use **Image > Adjustments > Desaturate** to convert a colour image to a greyscale image quickly. After converting, the lightness in the pixels remains the same, so differences in colour are still reflected. Desaturation is usually used for effect, though, rather than colour correction – for instance, taking a colour photo and making it look old.

The Auto Color option offers a fast and easy way to correct the colour in your image. When working towards perfecting an image, try this first.

Tweaking the colour levels

There are three options for tweaking the colour levels in a photo or image: **Image > Adjustments > Auto Color**, **Image > Adjustments > Color Balance**, and **Image > Adjustments > Variations**. Each can be used to improve the colour levels in an image. Sometimes this is all you need to get the colour just right; at other times you'll need to combine it with hue, saturation, brightness and contrast to get the perfect picture. Figure 2.5 shows the image menu and these choices.

2: Enhancing photos   41

Figure 2.5 Changing the hue can be used for effect or to correct colour in an image.

Photoshop doesn't know that exit signs are supposed to be red, or that the colour of a person's face shouldn't be green. Therefore, don't be surprised if you don't always get a perfect result.

Auto Color automatically adjusts the contrast and colour for the image by neutralising the midtones and clipping the black and white pixels in the image. This clipping of pixels and neutralising of tones is defined in the **Auto Correction Options** dialogue box accessed from **Image > Adjustments > Levels**, and by clicking the **Options** button in this dialogue box. For now, let Photoshop do what it thinks is best; as you get more experience with the program, with colours, and with optimising images, you can consider changing these defaults.

The second option for tweaking colour levels is the **Color Balance** command. To learn to use this, follow the steps outlined here.

1. Open an image from your hard drive or digital camera. Open the Peppers.jpg file from the Samples folder if an image isn't available.
2. Choose **Image > Adjustments > Color Balance**.
3. Drag the **Color Balance** dialogue box to an area of the work space where it won't cover up the image, and make sure the **Preview** box is ticked (see Figure 2.6).
4. Move the sliders on each of the colour bars to manipulate the colours in your image. For the Peppers.jpg image, move the **Magenta/Green** slider to –51 for a nice effect. Return it to zero. Move the **Yellow/Blue** slider to +58 and see the effect there too.
5. Checking **Preserve Luminosity** keeps the brightness levels intact; untick it to see how this affects the image.
6. Notice that **Midtones** is selected. Midtones are the 'middle' colours in the spectrum of colours in the image. Highlights are brighter colours, and shad-

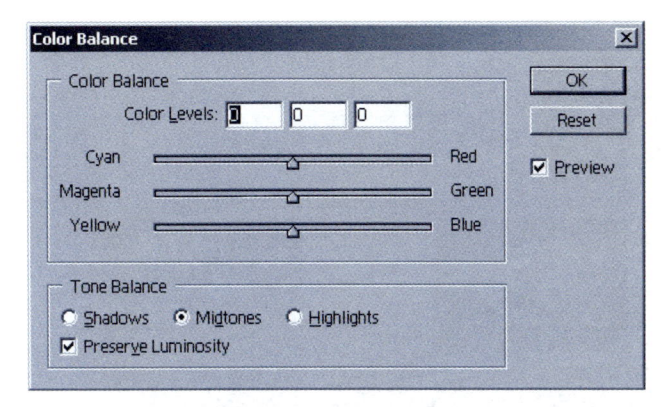

Figure 2.6 Use the Color Balance dialogue box to tweak colors.

ows are darker ones. If your image has lots of shadows or highlights, consider changing this setting; otherwise leave it at its default value.

7. Click **Cancel** when finished.

The **Variations** command also offers some great ways to enhance colours. This option shows you various versions of the image you are editing, and allows you to easily edit the image you have or choose one that's been automatically generated. If you see one in these options that you like, just select it from the top two pictures, and click OK. Figure 2.7 shows this tool in action.

To use this option, open up an image, choose **Image > Adjustments > Variations**, and look at the options. Select the one you like best – perhaps More Cyan or More Blue. The picture in the **Current Pick** rectangle at the

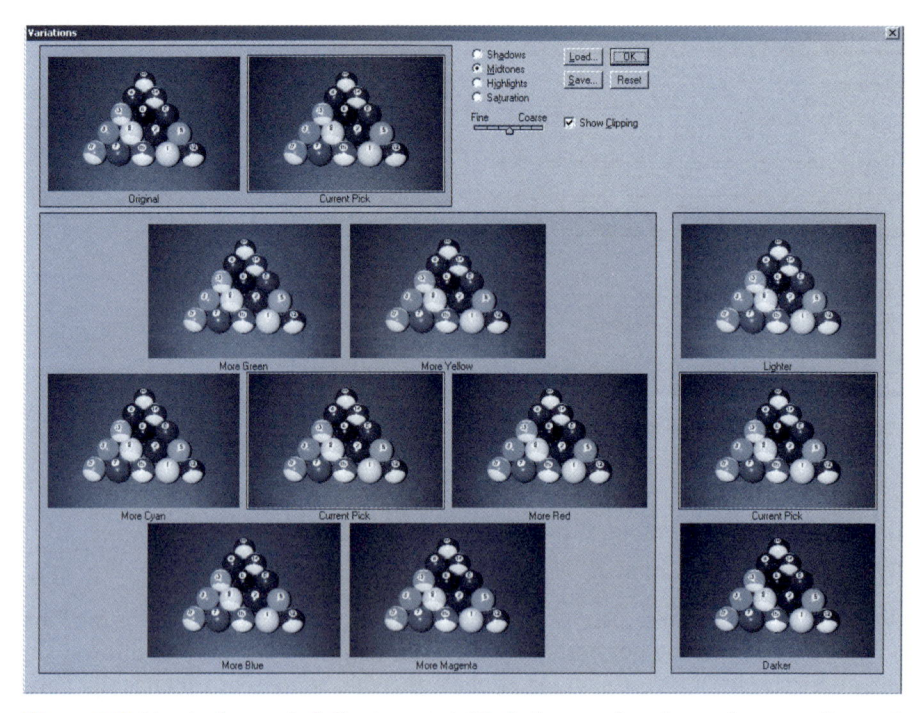

Figure 2.7 Use the **Image > Adjustments > Variations** tool to choose from or edit your image.

top shows the current configuration. When that's the way you want it, choose **OK**. You can reset all of the pictures by clicking on the picture in the **Original** rectangle at the top of the page.

2: Enhancing photos

As with all of the commands and dialogue boxes described so far, there are lots of other options; unfortunately, we don't have space to delve too deeply into them. Experiment with the options here to get a feel for what they do. When finished, select **Cancel** to choose not to apply the changes or select **OK** to apply them.

Creating instant photonegatives

The **Invert** command inverts the colours in an image. You can use this command to make a black and white image into a photonegative or to make a positive image from a scanned black and white negative. Although you can use the Invert command with colour photos and negatives, accurate colour negatives and images aren't produced. This command works well only with black and white photos and negatives. To use the Invert command, open an image and choose **Image > Adjustments > Invert**.

Minding the History palette

As mentioned in Chapter 1, the History palette is one of the default palettes in the workspace. This palette lists the changes you've made to your work during the current session and allows you to take snapshots of your work in progress. Snapshots should be taken when you are sure that you like the state of your work at the present time. The snapshot will serve as the baseline for future changes, and all snapshots are saved at the top of the History palette list.

The number of steps saved by default is 20. As steps 21 and above are performed, the first steps are erased from the palette. The default number of steps saved can be changed through the **Edit > Preferences > General** command.

You can always use Edit > Step Backward or Edit > Undo to retract anything you've just done.

Use the History palette to return to an earlier state and time, and to perform multiple undo commands.

To manually take a snapshot of your work:

1. Open the History palette from **Window > History** if it isn't already open, or drag it from the Palette Well if it's docked there.
2. Click the **New Snapshot** button located at the bottom of the History palette. It looks like a camera.
3. Scroll to the top of the History palette and find Snapshot 1. Double-click on it to rename it. Click here when you want to revert to this snapshot.
4. The icon next to the camera is the **Create new document from current state** option. Use this to create a new document for experimenting; this way, changes are not made to the current file.

Saving your work

Saving your work is covered in depth in Chapter 10, so in this section we'll just cover enough of the basics to get that file saved to the hard drive, so you can turn off your computer and do something else.

To save an image you've finished working on:

1. Select the **File > Save As** command.
2. From the **Save As** dialogue box, click the down arrow next to the **Look In** window, and locate the folder you've selected for saving files. I'd suggest the My Pictures folder or something similar.
3. In the **File Name** window, type in a descriptive name for the file. Try not to make it more than 15 characters or so, and stay away from special characters like *, &, %, $, @ and !.

4. Choose a file format. For saving a work in progress, use the Photoshop (PSD) format; for saving a photo for e-mailing, choose the JPEG format; and for saving line art or illustrations for e-mailing, choose the GIF format. For more information on file formats, refer to Chapter 10.
5. If prompted with compression options, accept the defaults and choose **OK**.

Remember, when working with files from the Samples folder, rename the file before saving. Otherwise, you'll be saving over the original file, which you won't want to do. Also, consider reducing the image size before saving. Reducing the image size greatly reduces the file size and the space it takes up on your computer. You can change the image size using **Image > Image Size**.

Summary

In this chapter you learned how to enhance a photo quickly and easily using Photoshop's automatic adjustments. You also learned how to open files from scanners, cameras and drives, as well as how to save your work when finished. In the next chapter, you'll learn more about editing photos.

Editing photos 3

Making a selection
Using the Magic Wand
Using the Lasso tool
Processing your selection
Transforming your selection
Blurring, sharpening and smudging
Dodging, burning and sponging
Cropping
Changing the colours
Using the Eyedropper
Using the Paint Bucket tool
Using the Gradient tool
Feathering
Cloning
Summary

There's a big difference between adjusting a photo's colour, hue, brightness and similar attributes, and actually editing the photo. When you adjust these attributes, you usually affect the entire image. Editing on the other hand often times has more to do with manipulating *parts* of a photo – removing an object in it, cropping it, and using effects such as blurring, sharpening, smudging, feathering and cloning. These effects can be applied to particular pieces of the image or to the entire image. To apply an effect to a part of the image requires that you select it first, so let's start this chapter by seeing how to make a selection using the selection tools.

Making a selection

You can use the selection tools to select a part of an image for editing. In Photoshop, there are several selection tools available, including the Marquee tools, the Lasso tools and the Magic Wand tool. Using these tools you can select parts of images by their colour, size and shape. In this section, you'll learn about the Magic Wand tool and the Lasso tools.

Using the Magic Wand

The **Magic Wand** tool lets you select a part of an image based on its colour. When you click on an image with this tool, a selection is automatically performed that consists of the pixels in the image that are similar in colour to those clicked on with the mouse. The pixels selected are also adjacent to the original pixels selected, and the tolerance level can be set from the Options bar so you can avoid selecting wildly across the entire image. Lessen the tolerance to tighten what colours should be selected, thus selecting smaller areas, or increase the tolerance, thus increasing the areas of colour selected.

3: Editing photos 51

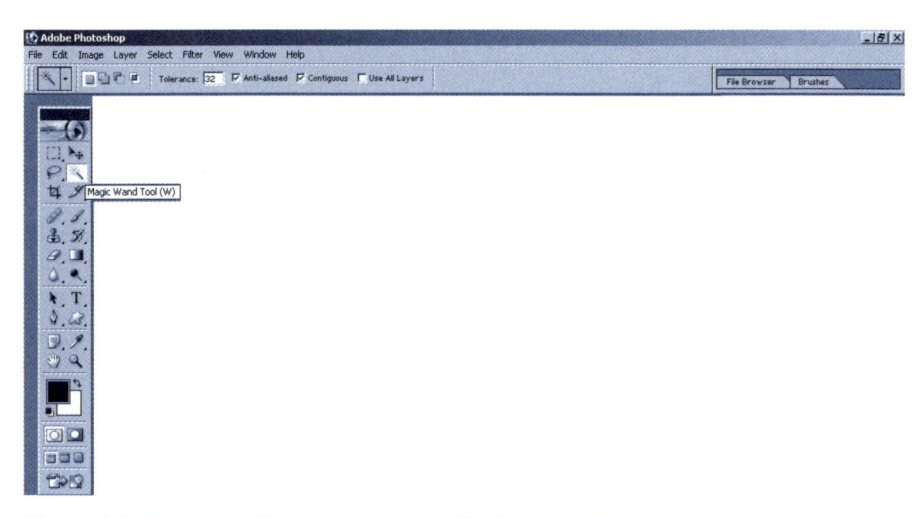

Figure 3.1 The Magic Wand is located in the Toolbox, and the Options bar changes when selected.

The Magic Wand tool is located in the Toolbox and is the second tool down on the right side. Once selected, the Options bar changes to reflect the choice. Figure 3.1 shows the Magic Wand tool and the changes to the Options bar.

In the Options bar there are several settings that can be configured. The Tolerance level is the most important, and the default is 32. This means that when you click on the image, the area that will be selected is an area that contains colours that are 32 shades lighter and 32 shades darker than the pixels originally selected with the mouse. You can increase this number to have more shades selected and decrease it for less, thus increasing or decreasing the selected area.

Let's give the Magic Wand tool a whirl:

1. Open any image that has distinct colours, such as the birdhouse shown in Figure 3.2. (I'm going to select the birdhouse using the Magic Wand tool, copy it from the image, and then place the birdhouse in another picture.)
2. Select the **Magic Wand** tool from the Toolbox by clicking on it once.
3. Click the mouse in the picture on the colour you want to select. In the case of the birdhouse, this would be green. Notice that the cursor is now a magic wand.
4. If you don't get the selection you desire, choose **Edit > Undo Magic Wand**. Then type in a new number for the **Tolerance** level, say 50. Experiment for a while to select as much area as possible.

Figure 3.2 Using the Magic Wand to select areas of similar colour.

5. When most of the object is selected, hold down the **Shift** key to select other parts of the object. Change the Tolerance level to 10 or 15 to select the smaller parts of the image that have yet to be selected. While using the **Shift** key, the cursor will be a magic wand with a plus sign, which indicates that whatever you select with it will be added to the previous selection.
6. Continue holding down the Shift key and clicking with the mouse until the entire object is selected. At any time, you can use the Undo command to go back one step.
7. Once you've selected the object, you can then use **Edit > Copy** to copy the selection.

Once the selection has been copied, you can paste it into any other image or to another area of the image you are working with. In this example, I copied it out of the original image and pasted it into the image shown in Figure 3.3.

You can get really creative with this tool. Imagine being able to cut out objects from an image or photograph and placing them somewhere else!

Using the Lasso tool

The **Lasso** tool is the second tool down on the left in the Toolbox. If you click on this icon and hold down the mouse for a second, you'll see the three options. There is the Lasso tool, the Polygonal Lasso tool, and the Magnetic Lasso tool. If you just click quickly on the icon once, you'll get whatever tool was last selected.

All of the tools are used in basically the same way: you use them to make free-hand selections, i.e you have to make the selection yourself.

*You can also deselect what has been selected by right-clicking on the object and choosing **Deselect**.*

Use what you know about zooming and using the Hand tool to get really precise with your selections.

Figure 3.3 Using the Magic Wand tool and **Edit > Copy** and **Edit > Paste** to edit a photo.

To use the Lasso tool in its most basic form, just choose it from the Toolbox, click next to the object you want to select, and try to draw around its edges with the lasso. You'll be drawing freehand, so this might be a little difficult at first, but you'll soon get the hang of it. You must hold down the mouse while selecting with the Lasso tool.

The **Polygonal Lasso** tool is similar to the Lasso tool, except that it draws straight lines, and it must be used to draw a polygon. Polygons are closed shapes, and can have as many sides as needed. To draw with this tool, click with the mouse where the line is to start, let go of the mouse, and then click again where you want the first line segment to be drawn. Let go of the mouse again, and click again for the next side or line segment. Continue in this manner until a closed polygon has been formed.

You can switch between the Lasso tool, which draws lines as you draw them with the mouse, to the Polygonal Lasso tool, which allows you to draw around an object using straight lines. To switch between these tools, hold down the mouse and click on the **Alt** key (PC) or the **Option** key (Mac).

Finally, the **Magnetic Lasso** tool can be used to draw around objects that are distinct from their backgrounds and contrast them highly. When using this tool, the selection border automatically snaps to the edge of the object you are trying to trace. When using this tool click often to create handles (control points) on the edge of the object. When clicking, the border will snap to the object you are selecting.

As with the Magic Wand, employ these tools with the Zoom and Hand tools for better precision.

Processing your selection

Once you've selected an area, you can process your selection in several different ways. The selected object can be cut, copied and/or pasted from the original image and added to other images, it can be moved within the same image, and new layers can even be created from it. (Although layers won't be covered until Chapter 6, a brief introduction is applicable here.)

The best way to learn about selecting and processing a selection is to do it yourself, so here is an example to follow:

1. Open a photo that contains an object you can easily trace around using the selection tools detailed in this section.
2. Use the Lasso, Polygonal Lasso and Magnetic Lasso tools to trace around the object.

3. Once the selection is complete, choose **Edit > Copy**.
4. Open a new file using **File > New**, and choose 1024 × 768.
5. Choose **Edit > Paste** to paste the selection into the new file. See Figure 3.4.
6. Now, use **File > Open** to open an existing image. Paste the selection into this new file using **Edit > Paste**. Click on the **Move** tool to move the pasted image to the desired location. Earlier, in Figure 3.3, the birdhouse was pasted using this technique on to an existing photo.
7. Return to the original picture, the one with the selected image. Make sure the Lasso tool is selected, then right-click on the selection.
8. From the drop-down list, select **Layer Via Copy**. A new layer will be created, which is simply just a copy of the object selected.
9. Select the **Move** tool, click on the object you just copied in step 8, and drag it to a new location in the image. This new layer is comprised of the selected object, and can be manipulated independently.

There are other ways to process a selection, although these seem to be the easiest and are a good place to start. As you progress through this book, you'll learn about other ways to manipulate a selection or create layers.

For all cases, use the **Esc** key or press the **Cancel** button in the Options bar to discard changes, or, press the **Enter** or **Return** keys or the **Commit** button on the Options bar to apply the changes.

3: Editing photos 57

Figure 3.4 Using **Edit > Paste** to paste a selected object.

Transforming your selection

There are several ways you can transform a selection once you've chosen it with the Lasso tools or the Magic Wand (or any other selection tool.) To see the Transform tools, click **Edit > Transform** and take a look at the drop-down list. There are several options:

- **Scale**
- **Rotate**
- **Skew**
- **Distort**
- **Perspective**
- **Rotate**
- **Flip**.

Each of these options provides handles around the selection so it can be stretched, rotated, scaled or otherwise distorted, as well as flipped horizontally or vertically and rotated a specific number of degrees.

To use these tools and to understand the differences between each of them, work through the following example:

1. Open a file that contains something easily traceable, and select the object in it using the selection tools. I'm tracing around the birdhouse used in Figures 3.2 and 3.3, because it's mostly rectangular and easy to select.

2. Choose **Edit > Transform** and select **Scale**. The Options bar changes to reflect this choice. Scale enlarges or reduces the size of the selection and is applied by dragging from the object's handles. Holding down the **Shift** key

You can transform a single layer or a selection using the Transform tools. To transform a layer, select it in the Layers palette first. To transform a selection, make the selection with one of the selection tools first. You can't transform a background layer. You'll learn more about layers in Chapter 6.

while dragging maintains proportion, as does dragging from the corners and not the sides. You can also scale numerically by typing in the height and width ratios in the Options bar. Click the lock in that bar to maintain proportion when resizing. Hit the **Esc** key so the changes to scale are not applied.

3. With the object still selected, choose **Edit > Transform** and select **Rotate**. To rotate the object manually, place the cursor outside of the bounding box that surrounds the object. The cursor becomes a curved two-headed arrow. Click and drag to rotate the object. Hold down the **Shift** key while dragging to reduce the rotation to 15 degrees. Rotate numerically by typing in new numbers for height and width in the Options bar. Press the **Esc** key so as not to apply the changes.

4. With the object still selected, choose **Edit > Transform** and select **Skew**. Skewing enables you to slant items vertically or horizontally. Drag outward or inward from the corner handles to change the object. Skew can be used to make the object seem to lean towards or away from the original location. You can also skew numerically by typing in numbers in the Options bar. Press the **Esc** key to discard the changes. See Figure 3.5.

5. With the object selected, choose **Edit > Transform** and then **Distort**. To distort the object drag from the various handles surrounding the object. You can also distort numerically from the Options bar. Press **Esc** to discard the changes. See Figure 3.5.

6. With the object selected, choose **Edit > Transform** and choose **Perspective**. Dragging from the handles changes the image by angling so that it looks like it's moving nearer or farther away. This can be done numerically as well, using the Options bar. Press the **Esc** key to discard changes. See Figure 3.5.

The object rotates around a centre point. Move the cursor inside the bounding box and click on the centre point. Drag this centre point to another area of the screen to create a new rotation point.

While looking at Figure 3.5, think about how those birdhouses could be added to trees to denote different types of perspective. The skewed one looks like it's on a slant, the perspective one looks like its way up in a tree, and the distorted one looks like it's being blown around in a storm.

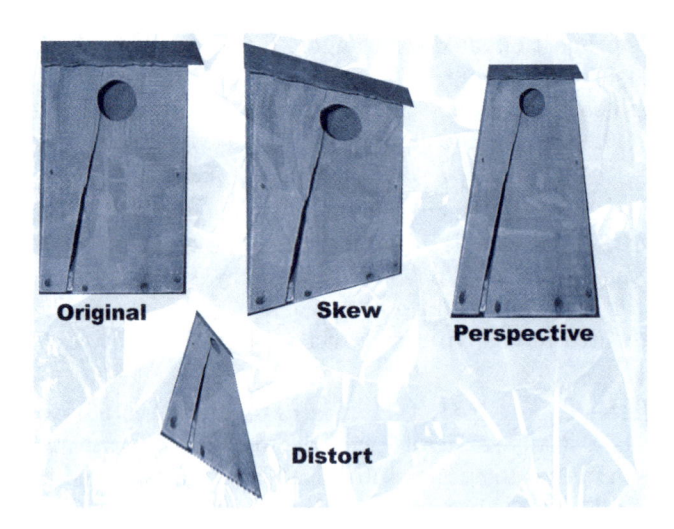

Figure 3.5 Examples of the Transform command.

7. Try the **Rotate** and **Flip** commands now. These commands enable you to rotate an image 90 or 180 degrees, or you can type in an amount in the Options bar. Flipping allows you to flip the object horizontally or vertically. Both of these tools can be used in combination with the other Transform tools.

The **Edit > Transform > Free Transform** lets you use all of these tools together, without having to select a separate command each time. To toggle between each of these tools use the following key combinations:

- Use the double-headed arrow outside the bounding box to rotate.
- Drag from any handle to scale.
- Hold down the **Alt** key (PC) or the **Options** key (Mac) while dragging to distort.
- Hold down the **Ctrl+Shift** keys (PC) or the **Command+Shift** keys (Mac) while dragging to skew.
- Hold down the **Ctrl+Alt+Shift** keys (PC) or the **Command+Option+Shift** keys (Mac) while dragging to apply perspective.

In all cases, use the **Esc** key or press the **Cancel** button in the Options bar to discard changes, or press the **Enter** or **Return** keys or choose the **Commit** button on the Options bar to apply the changes.

Blurring, sharpening and smudging

The Blur, Sharpen and Smudge tools are available in the Toolbox and are located seventh down on the left. You can see all three tools by clicking on the tool and holding down the mouse button for about a second. The **Blur** tool is the first one listed and is used to soften edges of objects or images, by allowing you to use a brush to manually cover over hard edges to reduce the detail in the image or object. The Blur tool can also be used to blend in images that stand out too much in a picture.

The **Sharpen** tool is the opposite of the Blur tool. It sharpens or enhances the effect of an image or an object, and is good for restoring edges that are not well defined and for bringing out images that have less than desirable edges. The **Smudge** tool smoothes edges and allows you to bleed in edges so the transition is even.

Each time you transform an image and commit that transformation, it loses a little clarity. Try to keep transformations to a minimum and perform multiple transformations before committing the changes.

To use and experiment with these tools, perform the following steps:

1. Open an image in Photoshop 7.0.
2. Click and hold down the mouse button on the **Blur/Sharpen/Smudge tool**, located in the Toolbox, seventh down on the left.
3. Choose the **Blur** tool.
4. From the Options bar, select a brush size by clicking on the down arrow next to the Brush choice. You'll use this brush to soften the corners of the image.
5. Click on the arrow next to **Strength**, and move the slider higher to blur more than the default, or lower to blur less. You'll have to experiment to determine what you need.
6. Click on the arrow next to **Mode**, and select **Normal** to blend the blur in using the default settings, choose **Lighten** or **Darken** to blur using lighter or darker effects, or choose **Hue**, **Saturation**, **Color** or **Luminosity** for additional blur effects. It is best to experiment with each type until you get the effect you want.
7. Using the mouse, drag over the areas to blur parts of the image. In the example of the birdhouse, I might choose to blur the edges of the birdhouse to make it seem to blend in with the tree better, so that it doesn't look too obvious that I added something to the image.

Try the same steps using the Sharpen and Smudge tools. Both of these are excellent ways to quickly add effect to an image. The Sharpen tool enhances edges, and if used repeatedly over the same area, seems to remove a part of the object. Use this tool sparingly to enhance edges or parts of objects, or use it liberally to add effect.

The Smudge tool distorts the image, and does so in the same way you could distort an image by rubbing you finger over wet paint or pencil drawings. Using this tool you can blur and distort the image at the same time, and apply an effect similar to watercolour by picking up colour in the area where you start dragging, and pushing it on to the area you move the mouse.

Dodging, burning and sponging

The **Dodge**, **Burn** and **Sponge** tools are located next to the Blur, Sharpen and Smudge tools in the Toolbox. They can be found seventh down on the right-hand side. The terms 'dodge' and 'burn' are taken from photography jargon and are techniques used to lighten or darken an image during the print process. Dodging is a technique in which light is held back to lighten an area of an image, while burning is a technique in which more light is added to make an area darker. You'll use these tools to apply this same effect.

The Sponge tool is a little different, and has to do with changing the colour saturation of an image. Use the Sponge tool to adjust strength and purity of colour.

To use these three tools:

1. Open any image.
2. If the image has multiple layers, select the layer to work on. For more information about layers, see Chapter 6. To work on the entire image and include all layers, don't do anything.
3. Click once and hold on the icon that holds the Dodge, Burn and Sponge tools. It is the seventh tool in the toolbox on the right-hand side. Select the **Dodge** tool.

*When any of these three tools is chosen, there is an option in the Options bar to select **All Layers**. When you select All Layers, the tool is applied to all of the layers in the image, otherwise it is applied only to the layer you are working on. More about layers in Chapter 6.*

4. From the Options bar, select a brush size by clicking on the down arrow next to **Brush**. You'll use this brush to lighten parts of the image.
5. Click on the arrow next to **Exposure** and move the slider higher to lighten more than the default, or lower to lighten less. You'll have to experiment to determine what you need. Lightening in this manner leaves the colour intact, but seems to remove light from it.
6. Click on the arrow next to **Range**, and select **Midtones** to lighten using the default settings and lighten midtone colours; **Shadows** to lighten shadows in the image; or **Highlights** to lighten highlights in your image. Once again, it is best to experiment until you get the effect you want.
7. Using the mouse, drag over the areas to lighten.

Try the same steps using the Burn and Sponge tools. Both of these are excellent ways to quickly add effect to an image. The Burn tool darkens the image in the same manner as the Dodge tool lightens it. The Sponge tool is a little different.

The Sponge tool changes the colour in an image only subtly by making the colour 'truer', or more pure. The more you drag the tool across an area, the more effect is applied. The options for the Sponge tool in the Options bar include Brush, Mode and Flow, and are used in a similar way to the Dodge and Burn options.

Cropping

Cropping has to be one of the most useful tools available. This tool allows you to select part of an image and remove the rest of the image that isn't selected. Cropping allows you to centre people in photos, remove parts of photos, focus

*As you work with various Options bars, you'll change the default settings for them. Remember that you can always revert back to the default settings by right-clicking on the far left icon in the Options bar and choosing **Reset Tool**.*

on only one object in a photograph, such as a building, cloud or other object not specifically part of the original thought when the photo was taken, and more.

To use the cropping tools:

1. Open an image you'd like to crop.
2. From the Toolbox, select a **Marquee** tool. These tools are located under the first icon on the left side in the Toolbox. Click and hold down the mouse button to see all four tools. There are choices for Rectangular Marquee tool, Elliptical Marquee tool, Single Row Marquee tool, and Single Column Marquee tool. Choose the **Rectangular Marquee** tool.
3. Click on the image and drag to select the area to crop. Once selected, let go of the mouse.
4. Move or resize the box using the mouse by dragging from the bounding box.
5. When finished, choose **Image > Crop**.

Besides cropping with the Marquee tools and the **Image > Crop** command, you can also use the Crop tool in the Toolbox. It is the third tool on the left-hand side. To use this tool:

1. Click **Edit > Undo** to undo the last crop command.
2. Click on the **Crop** tool in the Toolbox, and drag the mouse over the area you want to keep.
3. Resize, move, rotate or otherwise manipulate the selection until the desired effect is achieved.
4. Hit **Enter** or **Return** or choose another tool and click **Crop** to apply the crop, or press **Escape** to cancel.

When you use the Elliptical Marquee tool, an ellipse will be drawn around the selection, but when cropped, the selection will not be cropped as an ellipse. It crops with a rectangle, leaving the elliptical selection still marked.

Changing the colours

There are three tools available that can be used quite easily to change the colour of an entire image, the colour of a part of an image, the colour of a shape, page or new file, and even apply a gradient to an image. These tools are the Eyedropper, the Paint Bucket tool and the Gradient tool.

Using the Eyedropper

Sometimes you just need to touch up a small area of a photo, and you need to match the colours exactly. For instance, you might want to remove a blemish from an older photo, remove wrinkles or dark colours under a subject's eyes, touch up the hedges that should have been trimmed, or cover over some other flaw in a photograph or image. The **Eyedropper** tool allows you to do this quite easily by enabling you to match a colour from another part of the photo, and use that colour to paint over the unwanted parts of the image.

Take a look at Figure 3.6. It is a picture of two carved wooden art pieces, and they are propped up on the fireplace mantle. If you want to send this picture to an art gallery, your Aunt Bessie, or a colleague, you'll want to clean it up a bit. Looking more closely at the photo, you might notice there are flaws in it. The paint has been sloppily applied to the wall, and some of it is on the grout by the brick. The wall itself has a crack in it too. These flaws can be removed (actually, covered over) using the Eyedropper tool.

To use this tool:

1. Open a photo or image that needs to be touched up. In this example, I'm going to 'paint' over the flaws in the wall.

3: Editing photos

Figure 3.6 Locating blemishes in a photo.

2. Locate the Eyedropper tool; it is the tenth one down on the right in the Toolbox. (It's also shown in Figure 3.7.) Click on the icon and hold down the mouse button to see the three available tools: the Eyedropper tool, the Color Sampler tool and the Measure tool. Select the **Eyedropper** tool.

The foreground colour is shown in the Toolbox at the bottom. Click in various areas of the image to see how the foreground colour in this Toolbox changes.

3. Click the mouse (which is now the Eyedropper tool) on an area of the photograph that contains the colour you'd like to paint with or apply to the picture. In my example, that's the brown grout colour. I'm going to use that colour to paint over and hide the sloppy white painting on the mantle. The foreground colour will change to this colour.

4. Select the Brush tool; it's fourth down on the right in the Toolbox. (It's also shown in Figure 3.7.) Click and hold down the mouse button to see the choices. From the Options bar, select a brush from the **Brush** drop-down list that is the right size for applying the new colour to the image. Configure any other settings here too.

5. Using the Brush tool, drag the mouse over the part of the image you want to change.

6. While painting over the blemishes in the photo, you'll probably need to take several more Eyedropper colour samples. You can toggle between the Eyedropper tool and any other painting tool by clicking and holding the **Alt** key.

Using the Paint Bucket tool

The Paint Bucket is just what you think it is; it's a bucket full of paint that you can 'spill' on to a selection or part of an image. In fact, when you choose the **Paint Bucket** tool the cursor changes to a can of paint that is tipped to one side. The Paint Bucket tool can be accessed from the Toolbox, and is the sixth tool down on the right side. Click and hold down the mouse button on this icon to see the choices: Gradient tool and Paint Bucket tool.

When the Paint Bucket tool is used, a sample is taken of the colour in the area you've clicked on. Any pixels that are touching this sample area will be changed to the new colour in the Paint Bucket.

To see how the Paint Bucket tool works in its most basic form, do the following:

1. Go to **File > New** and choose 1024 × 768 from the **Preset Sizes**; for **Mode**, choose **RGB**; and for **Contents**, choose **White**. Click **OK**.
2. From the Toolbox, locate **Foreground and Background colors**. They are near the bottom of the toolbox and are squares. See Figure 3.7.
3. Double-click on the **foreground** icon. From the **Color Picker** dialogue box that opens, choose a new colour that you want to use in your new file. Click **OK**.
4. Select the **Paint Bucket** tool.
5. Click the mouse inside the new file to fill it with the new colour.

You can also fill shapes with colour, as well as selections or parts of images. To understand how the Paint Bucket tool works with an image, experiment by following these steps:

1. Open an image that has an area you want to fill with colour. I shall use the picture in Figure 3.6 and the Paint Bucket tool to 'repaint' the wall.
2. Select a foreground colour and then the **Paint Bucket** tool. (I'm going to paint my wall blue.)
3. From the Options bar, make sure **Foreground** is chosen for the **Fill**, and select an opacity. Opacity is how 'see-through' the new colour will be. When painting, 100% opacity puts the paint on thickly, while anything less will

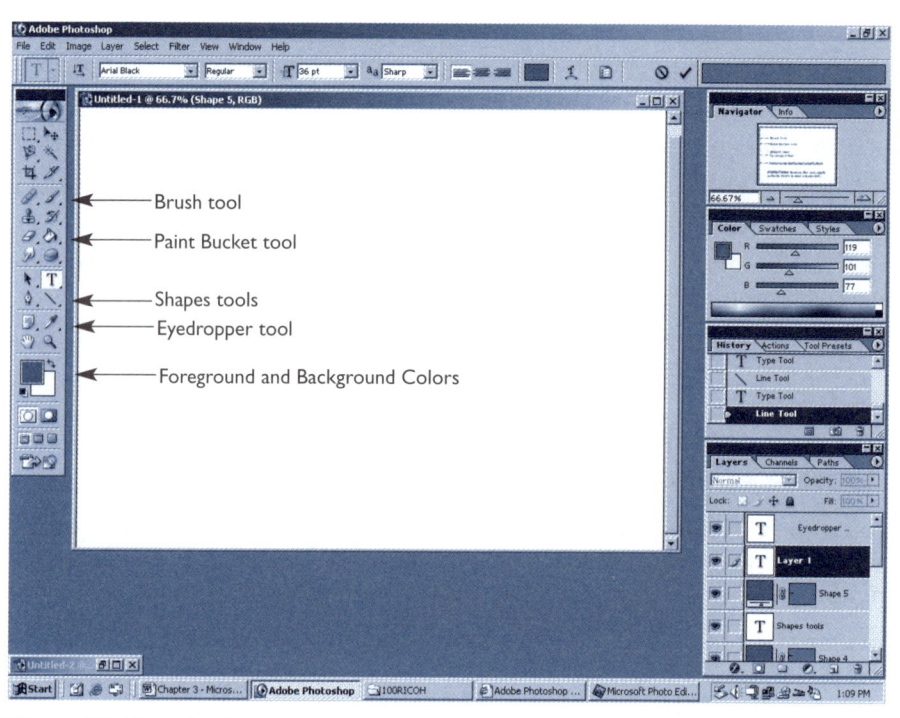

Figure 3.7 Photoshop's painting tools.

appear more transparent. When texture needs to show through, consider using a lower opacity; doing so will let the background come through slightly and will enhance the effect. See Figure 3.8.

4. From the Options bar, raise or lower the **Tolerance** to specify how similar a pixel must be in order to be filled with the foreground colour. A high number (up to 255) fills pixels with a broader range; a smaller number (zero) fills pixels with tighter colour requirements.

5. Click inside the areas to fill. Use the Eyedropper tool to fill in areas missed, or undo the Paint Bucket command and reset the options. Figure 3.8 shows my final image, which has also been cropped and adjusted, and is now ready to go to the art agency.

Using the Gradient tool

The **Gradient** tool is a gradual blend of colours that can be applied to an entire image, a layer or a selection. Gradients offer easy ways to create a background for a project or image, or to apply colour effects to a selected part of the image.

To see what a gradient is, what preset gradients are available, and how gradients are applied, follow these steps:

1. Open a new file from **File > New**. Choose 1024 × 768, white background, and RGB colour.
2. Select the **Gradient** tool; it's the sixth one down the Toolbox on the right-hand side. Click and hold down the mouse button on the icon to choose it from the available tools in this list.

Figure 3.8 Using the Paint Bucket tool.

3. From the Options bar, click the down arrow next to the gradient sample to see what gradients are available. Click the right arrow in this box to see more options. See Figure 3.9.

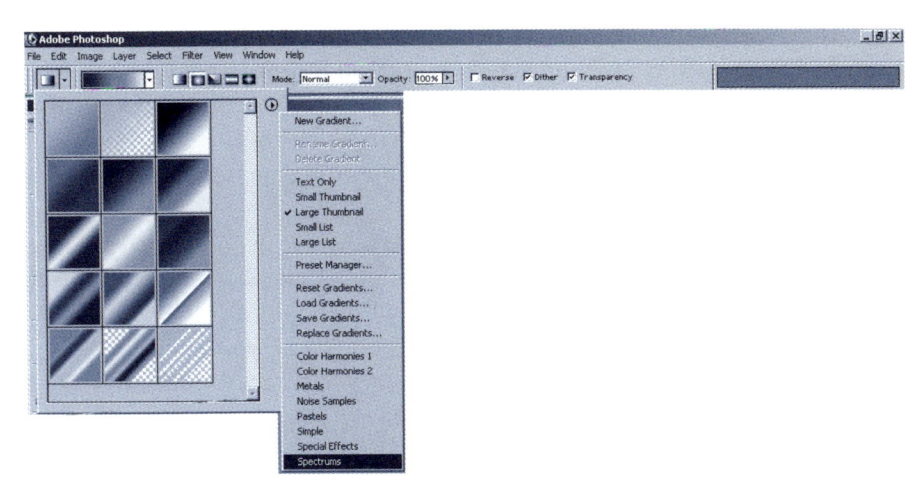

Figure 3.9 Gradient options.

4. If you want to, change how you will view the gradients in the Options bar. I prefer **Large Thumbnail**, as shown in Figure 3.9.
5. Choose **Color Harmonies 1**, **Color Harmonies 2**, **Metals**, **Noise Samples** and the other options shown in Figure 3.9 to browse through and look at all of the available gradients. Click **OK** in any dialogue boxes that appear. You can always revert back to the default by selecting **Reset Gradients** from this list.
6. Choose a gradient by double-clicking on it.

7. From the Options bar, choose **Linear**, **Radial**, **Angle**, **Reflected** or **Diamond** for a pattern. Linear blends in a straight line; Radial blends in a circle; Angle blends in an anticlockwise motion; Reflected uses reflections of linear gradients; and Diamond blends in a diamond pattern.
8. From the Options bar, select opacity and blending mode. You'll have to experiment to get the effect you want.
9. Select **Reverse** to reverse the colours in the gradient; select **Dither** to create a smoother blend of the colours with less visible bands; or select **Transparency** to create a transparency mask for the fill (this has to do with opacity and fill, and enables you to fade out the transparency).
10. Apply the gradient by clicking and dragging with the mouse. Begin where you want the gradient to begin, and let go where you want the gradient to end. Note that this has to do with the gradient pattern and not the selected area. The gradient will be applied to a selected area.

You can apply a gradient over an entire image and blend it in with the image by lowering the opacity settings.

You can apply gradients to selections as well as entire images; they don't have to be applied only to new files. However, when creating a logo, artwork for an invitation, a sign, a symbol or similar items, creating a background with a gradient on it can be a great place to start. To apply a gradient to a selection, use the **Marquee** tools to select the part of the image to apply the gradient to, or choose a layer from the **Layers** palette. (See Chapter 6 for more about layers.)

Feathering

Feathering is the process of smoothing edges of selections by blurring the boundary between the selection and the rest of the image. Feathering is set numerically, and the larger the number, the more blur or softening you get.

Feathering options are available from the Options bar when any of the Marquee or Lasso tools are selected.

Using the feathering options is simple: just choose any of the Marquee or Lasso tools, then type in a number between 0 and 250 in the **Feather** box in the Options bar. Then, use the tool to select an object. Feathering can also be applied using **Select > Feather** if an object has already been selected. Feathering is noticeable when the selection is cut, copied, moved or filled.

Feathering is most often used when removing an object or person from one photo and placing it in another. By softening the edges around the object you've selected, you can lessen the hard edges created by the selection tools, making the transition less noticeable. You can also use feathering to place a blurred or foggy effect around a flower or other object.

Cloning

The Clone Stamp tool, located in the Toolbox, fifth down on the right-hand side, can be used to clone objects, colours and parts of images. This is one of my favourite tools. Using this tool you can create your own twin, make a garden with only a few flowers a garden of 100 identical ones, and match colours in a similar way to using the Eyedropper tool.

To see the power in this tool, do the following:

1. Open an image with an item you'd like to clone.
2. Select the **Clone Stamp** tool from the Toolbox by clicking and holding on the icon and selecting it from the list of tools.

3. From the Options bar, select a brush, brush size, a blending mode, and other specifics.
4. By default, the **Aligned** box is selected. This means that you can release the mouse button while using the tool without losing your reference point and thus cloned pixels are applied continuously (see step 5). Leave this setting selected for now.
5. Hold down the **Alt** key and click once on the object or colour to clone; this is the reference or sampling point.
6. Move the cursor to another area of the image and hold down the mouse and drag. You'll see both the cursor and the reference point. As you move the cursor, objects under the reference point will be recreated.

Summary

In this chapter you learned how to select parts of images for editing using the Marquee and Lasso tools. Once selected, you were able to process and transform those selections by skewing, distorting, blurring, dodging, burning, smudging, cropping and filling with colour or gradients. You also learned how to clone and feather selections.

Creating art 4

Opening a canvas
Selecting the colours
Drawing lines
Using the Pencil tool
Picking a paintbrush
Erasing
Drawing shapes
Adjusting the size
Summary

Photoshop 7.0 isn't just for digital pictures; it can be used to create original artwork too. In this chapter, I'll introduce you to some of the art tools available for creating original artwork, including using a pencil, using brushes and erasing, and drawing different types of lines and shapes. You can combine these tools to create logos, T-shirt designs, flyers, invitations, 'for sale' signs, and more. You can even use these tools to touch up photos, remove or brush over objects you don't want in the picture, and remove blemishes and wrinkles from faces. The sky's the limit!

Opening a canvas

Before we can get started, let's open our canvas. Really, this is just a file we're going to open to work on, but we'll call it a canvas for now. Click on **File > New** to bring up the **New** dialogue box shown in Figure 4.1.

Type in a name for your new file; for this chapter, name it '*Art*'. Click the down arrow next to the **Preset Sizes** window and choose 1024 × 768. The **Width** and **Height** will show the new dimensions, and the default **Resolution** is 72 pixels per inch. Those settings are fine for now. (Refer to Chapter 1 for more information about pixels, resolutions and other file attributes.) The other sizes are simply other choices; I prefer 1024 × 768 for creating artwork because it's big and offers enough room for experimenting.

For **Contents**, there are three choices: **White** gives your canvas a white background; **Background Color** allows you to choose a background colour; and **Transparent** gives a transparent background. If you choose Background Colour, the canvas will be automatically filled with the colour that is assigned to the background colour in the Toolbox. If you choose Transparent, the colour of the canvas will be checked. When transparent images are created, the artwork you add to the canvas will not have any background at all. Artwork drawn to transparent backgrounds can then be selected and used on Web pages or added to other artwork or images, and the background Web page or image will show underneath it. You'll learn more about this in later chapters, especially when we begin talking about layers.

For our beginning artwork, choose **White** background and **RGB Color**. RGB Color is only one of several choices though; in the next section, you'll learn about the other colour modes.

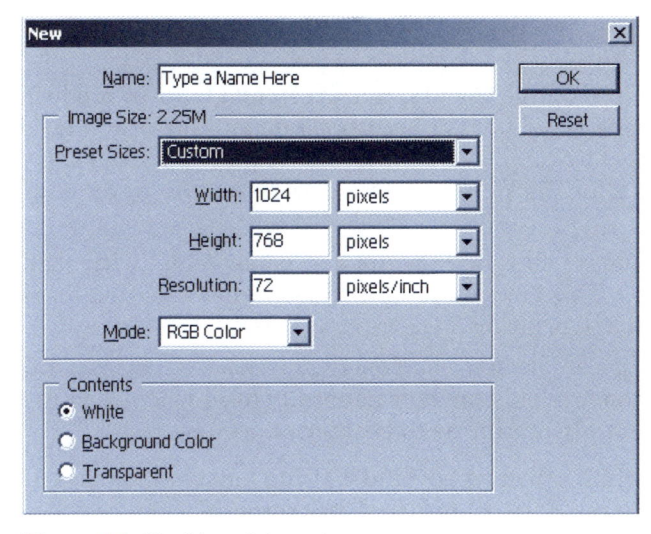

Figure 4.1 The New dialogue box.

Each time you create a new file, you'll need to choose a setting that fits your needs.

Setting the colours

When creating a new file, there are several options for colour **Mode**. You chose RGB this time, but there are other choices. How do you know when to use a specific mode? The following list briefly describes each and their purpose.

- **Bitmap** – this mode uses different levels of black and white to produce colours in an image. Bitmaps can be used for printing photos with low resolution, but other options are better.
- **Grayscale** – this mode uses up to 256 different shades of grey and is often chosen when working with black and white photos or creating black and white artwork.
- **RGB Color** – this mode uses three colours, red, green and blue, to produce up to 16.7 million colours on screen. It is Photoshop's default for new images and is also the system used by computer monitors to display colours. This is the best option for images for the Web, for working with photos, or for editing images.
- **CMYK Color** – this mode is based on how ink and paper relate with each other and the human eye. This mode is generally used when creating four-colour separated artwork and printing on to paper.
- **Lab Color** – this mode has a lightness component, a green–red component, and a blue–yellow component. This mode is generally used when working with photos from CDs, and when printing to PostScript printers.

Now that you have a new white canvas ready and waiting for some colour artwork, let's set some colours. Foreground and background colours were introduced briefly in Chapter 3, but will be introduced in more depth here. The

Set Foreground Color and **Set Background Color** tools are located towards the bottom of the Toolbox, and show the currently configured colours. The **Color** palette is located on the right-hand side of the workspace and can be shown or hidden using the **Window > Color** command. All of these tools help you configure the colours in your work.

To use these tools, do the following:

1. Click on the **Set Foreground Color** icon in the Toolbox. From the **Color Picker**, move the sliders to locate the desired colour.
2. From the Color Picker you can also type in numbers for colour, select only colours for use on the Web, and even create custom colours. Web colours are created from 216 colours that are supported by all Web browsers; to select only Web colours, place a tick in the Only Web Colors checkbox. If you are creating images for a website, tick the **Only Web Colors** checkbox to guarantee that viewers will see the colours you expect them to. To create custom colours, click the **Custom** button.
3. Click in the **Custom Colors** dialogue box, and in the colour window click or slide to browse through various colours. You can match any colour here. In larger printing shops, designers match customer's colours exactly using colour schemes from books and industry standards. Pantone colours are an example of this. These industry-standard colours are what allow companies to match colours exactly on business cards, signs and flyers, and also allow them to get the same colour output from different printers. Click **Cancel** to exit the dialogue box.
4. Click on the **Set Background Color** icon in the Toolbox. Notice that the options are the same as for foreground colour. Click **Cancel** .

*To match a colour on an image, move the mouse outside the **Color Picker** dialogue box. The cursor will change to the **Eyedropper** tool, where you can take a sample and have it automatically matched inside the Color Picker.*

You can also change the foreground and background colours from the Color palette:

1. Click on the **Set Foreground Color** icon in the Color Palette. Move the sliders for R, G and B to create new colours. Notice how the icon changes colour to reflect this.

2. Click on the **Set Background Color** icon in the Color Palette. Move the sliders for R, G and B to create new colours. Notice how the icon changes colour to reflect this.

3. Click the **Swatches** tab, and click on the colours there. Notice that the foreground colours changes. You can see these tabs as well as the additional options in Figure 4.2. Use these additional options to change the sliders that are shown in the Colour from RGB to any other listed Palette.

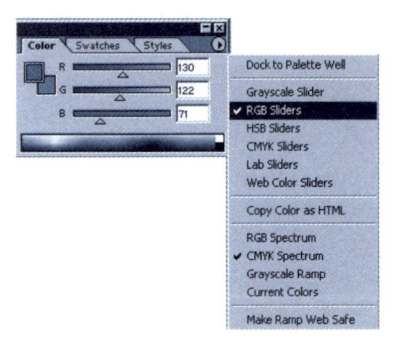

Figure 4.2 Additional Options from the Color palette.

Of course, Photoshop 7.0 is full of ways to choose and perfect colours in an image, and this is just an introduction. So what's the importance of foreground and background colours anyway? You'll see when we start drawing lines, next.

Drawing lines

There are several tools for drawing lines, the most popular being the **Pencil** and the **Brush** tools. Both of these tools are located in the Toolbox and are the fourth tool down on the right-hand side. Click and hold on this icon to see both the Pencil tool and the Brush tool choices. As with other tools in the Toolbox, the Options bar changes to reflect the choice made. The Options bar offers choices for brush type and size, opacity, mode, and more. Of course, drawing lines has to go hand in hand with erasing them, so in this section we'll talk about the **Eraser** tools too.

Using the Pencil tool

When you draw with either the Pencil tool or the Brush tool, you'll draw with the foreground colour. As you would suspect, the Pencil tool draws with hard lines, just like a real pencil does. However, with the help of opacity settings, you can configure the Pencil mark to be dark and heavy, or light. You can also draw with really large pencils by changing the options in the Options bar.

To use the Pencil tool:

1. Select the **Pencil** tool from the Toolbox. It is the fourth down on the right-hand side. Click and hold on the icon to select it from the resulting list.
2. Click on the canvas and drag the mouse to draw the line. The line is drawn using the foreground colour.

3. Change the foreground colour to black and draw another line.
4. From the Options bar, click the down arrow by the **Brush** options, and choose a larger brush by double-clicking on it in the drop-down choices.
5. Draw another line using the new brush.
6. From the Options bar, change the **Opacity** settings from 100% to 50% by either moving the slider or typing in a new number, and draw another line. Change it again to 25% and repeat.
7. Change the **Opacity** back to 100%, and this time just click once with the mouse to create circles or small pieces of a line.
8. There are several blending modes to select from, and these are addressed in Chapter 7. If you've read that chapter already, feel free to experiment with those options here.
9. Place a tick in the **Auto Erase** checkbox in the Options bar. Change the background colour to white, the same colour as the background of the canvas. Click on one of the lines you've already drawn, then drag the mouse over it. Watch the lines disappear. Actually, you are simply drawing white (the background colour) over the existing lines. Now, draw a line on an empty area of the workspace; the Pencil tool draws using the foreground colour again.
10. Change the background colour to red. Draw a line in an empty area of the canvas. Next, click on a line and trace over the top of it. When drawing on an empty area, the foreground colour is used. When tracing over a line that has been drawn using the foreground colour, the background color is used.
11. To draw a straight line, click the mouse where you want the line to begin, and hold down the **Shift** key while dragging. Instead of drawing freehand, you'll draw a straight line. Continue to hold down the **Shift** key while drag-

ging if you want another line to be drawn where you left off. If you want the new line to be independent of the last one drawn, release the **Shift** key, click the mouse again, and then select the **Shift** key while dragging.

Picking a paintbrush

Using the Brush tool is pretty much the same as using the Pencil tool, except there are two additional options on the Options bar when the Brush tool is chosen – **Flow** and **Enable Airbrush**. When using the Brush tool, you can configure how much 'paint' you want on the canvas by setting the flow. Do you want a heavy flow, a medium flow or a light flow? The Airbrush option can be enabled to offer a spray paint effect instead of a brush effect on the canvas.

To experiment with brushes and brush options:

1. Select the **Brush** tool from the Toolbox. It is the fourth down on the right-hand side. Click and hold on the icon to select it from the resulting list.
2. Click on the canvas and drag the mouse to draw the line. The line is drawn using the foreground colour.
3. Change the foreground colour to green and draw another line.
4. From the Options bar, click the down arrow by the **Brush** options, and choose a larger brush by double-clicking on it in the drop-down choices. There are literally hundreds of brushes. See Figure 4.3. Notice that I like the Large Thumbnail view, but that isn't the default, so your screen might look different. On the canvas, I've painted with Brush 74, which is a leaf. This would make a nice background for an autumn party invitation, a nursery logo, or even added lightly over a photograph.

If your green shows up as grey, you selected Grayscale mode or Bitmap mode instead of RGB color mode. You can change it to RGB from Image > Mode > RGB. Other modes are available as well. If there are multiple layers, you'll be prompted to flatten the layers before continuing, which will affect editing and layer composition.

Photoshop 7

*In the Brush palette in step 4, click the right arrow to see additional brush options. Square brushes look good, as do special effect and calligraphy brushes. Click **OK** if prompted to switch palettes; you can always switch back by selecting **Default**. See Figure 4.3.*

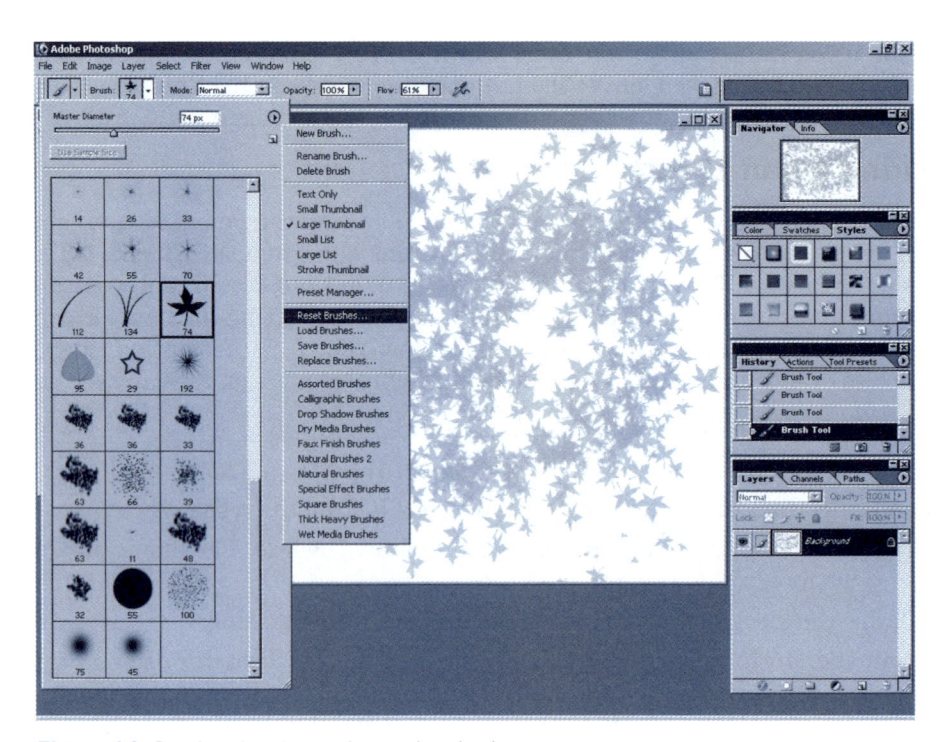

Figure 4.3 Brushes, brushes and more brushes!

5. Draw another line using the new brush; this time hold down the **Shift** key while drawing to create a straight line. Hold down the mouse button in one place to apply additional paint to the canvas, and to make the painting heavier.
6. From the Options bar, change the **Opacity** settings from 100% to 50% by either moving the slider or typing in a new number, and draw another line. Change it again to 25% and repeat. Change the Opacity back to 100%.
7. From the Options bar, change the **Flow** settings from 100% to 50% by either moving the slider or typing in a new number, and draw another line. Change it again to 25% and repeat. Flow determines how fast the paint will be applied. Return the number to 100%.
8. There are several blending modes to select from, and these are addressed in Chapter 7. If you've read that chapter already, feel free to experiment with those options here.
9. Click the **Airbrush** option on the Options bar. This changes the brush you are using to an airbrush. Airbrushes spray paint rather than brushing it on, and holding down the mouse while using the tool is the same as holding down the nozzle on a spray paint can. The longer you spray in one place, the more paint it applies.

Although we've been drawing and painting on a blank canvas, you can use the Brush tool for lots of other purposes. For instance, you can use the Brush tool to spray out a bird from a picture, a person from a beach photo, or colour from an object. The Brush tool can also be used to touch up photos, soften edges of selections, and touch up computer-generated artwork.

Erasing

Erasing isn't only used to erase pencil or brush strokes. The Eraser tools can be used for lots of other purposes. There are three Eraser tools available: the **Eraser** tool, the **Background Eraser** tool and the **Magic Eraser** tool. They are located in the Toolbox sixth down on the right-hand side. Just click and hold as you do with other tools, and select the one you want.

The Eraser tool simply erases. When erasing with this tool, the colour of the pixels changes to the background colour. This means that if you have green paint on a light background, and you use the Eraser tool to erase the green paint, the light background will show instead. If there is nothing underneath but a transparent layer, the Eraser tool erases to that layer.

The Background Eraser tool lets you erase colour on a canvas to transparency no matter what is underneath it. This tool allows you to erase everything in the background of an object and leave the foreground intact.

The Magic Eraser tool automatically erases all coloured pixels that match the colour you choose to erase. For instance, if you have a picture of land and sky, you can click on the sky using the Magic Eraser tool, and all of the sky will be erased to transparency. This is useful when you want to use only part of a photo or image, and you want to delete the rest.

Let's experiment with these Eraser tools.

1. Open a photo or other image. Select the **Eraser** tool from the Toolbox.
2. The Eraser tool erases by covering over the part of the image you want to erase with the background colour configured in the Color Palette or the

Toolbox. Change the background colour to match the background of your image, or whatever colour should be behind the object you are erasing.

3. Drag the mouse over the area to erase. The object won't actually be erased; it will simply be covered over with the background colour you've chosen. Notice from the Options bar that you can select Brush size, Opacity, Flow, and other attributes.
4. Choose the **Background Eraser** tool next.
5. Configure the brush from the Options bar. You'll have several options, including the diameter of the brush, the hardness of the brush, and brush spacing. It's best to start by choosing a suitable diameter, accepting the defaults, and then making changes as needed.
6. Choose a **Limits** mode for erasing, either **Contiguous** to erase areas that contain the sampled colour and are connected, or **Noncontiguous** to erase the sampled colour where it occurs under the brush.
7. Set the **Tolerance** level by moving the slider or by typing in a number. Lower levels limits what will be erased to colours very similar to the sampled colour (where you click first), and higher numbers will erase a broader range of colours.
8. If you need to prevent the areas that match the foreground colour from being erased, select **Protect Foreground Color**.
9. Drag the mouse over the areas to erase.
10. Choose the **Magic Eraser** tool from the Toolbox. The Magic Eraser tool erases colours that are similar without having to drag the mouse. Like the Background Eraser tool, you can configure **Tolerance** and **Contiguous** or **Noncontiguous**, to erase in the manner you want.

Here's a neat trick to match the colour you want, just in case you missed it earlier. Click on the **Set Background Color** *icon in the Toolbox. When the* **Color Picker** *dialogue box appears, move the cursor outside the dialogue box. The cursor will change to the Eyedropper tool. Click anywhere to choose a colour to match. The exact colour will be selected automatically in the Color Picker dialogue box. Click* **OK**.

11. Click on the image in an area of colour. You might have to click more than once to erase everything you need. Don't forget that you can zoom in too, and change the size and type of the brush.

Figure 4.4 shows a before-and-after picture. I've used the Eraser tools, the Paint Bucket tool, and some speciality brushes to change the outdoor picture of a palm into an indoor picture of an aquarium awaiting some fish.

Drawing shapes

Photoshop offers lots of shapes that you can add to an image. These shapes are located in the Toolbox and are the ninth tool down on the right-hand side. When you click and hold on this icon, you can choose from several available Shape tools:

- **Rectangle** tool
- **Rounded Rectangle** tool
- **Ellipse** tool
- **Polygon** tool
- **Line** tool
- **Custom Shape** tool.

As with the other tools in the Toolbox, the Options bar changes to reflect the choice. There are several options including how multiple shapes will interact with each other, whether or not the shape should be of fixed size, proportional or unconstrained, and what colour the inside of the shape should be. Before we get too far into all that, let's learn to draw some shapes first.

Figure 4.4 Transplanting a palm using the Eraser, Paint Bucket and Brush tools.

1. Click and hold down the **Shape** tool in the Toolbox to see the options. Choose the first option, the **Rectangle** tool.
2. Click and drag on the canvas to create the rectangle. It will fill with the colour configured on the Options bar.
3. To change the colour of the inside of the rectangle, click the **Colour** option in the Options bar, and choose a new colour from the **Color Picker**.
4. Draw another rectangle, this time holding down the **Shift** key while dragging. This enables you to draw a perfect square instead of a rectangle. (When holding down the **Shift** key with the Ellipse tool, you'll draw a perfect circle instead of an ellipse.)
5. Choose **Window > Workspace > Reset Palette Locations**. (For this exercise, you'll need to be able to see the Layers palette.)
6. Create several more rectangles and squares, and watch what happens in the Layers palette. As each new shape is created, so is a new layer. Although you don't know much about layers yet, this is pretty significant. This enables you to work with each shape independently of the other, and the layers themselves are independent as well.
7. Creating a new layer each time a shape is added is the default. However, you can change this default behaviour from the Options bar by choosing **Add To Shape Area**, **Subtract From Shape Area**, **Intersect Shape Areas**, and **Exclude Overlapping Shape Areas**.
    - **Add To Shape Area** places the new shape on the same layer as the preceding shape. Both combine to form one shape.
    - **Subtract From Shape Area** removes a part of the first shape where the second shape overlaps.

- **Intersect Shape Areas** removes both shapes except for where they overlap.
- **Exclude Overlapping Shape Areas** removes only where the two shapes overlap.

8. Styles can be applied to the new shape(s) too. Click on the down arrow next to the **Style** button in the Options bar as shown in Figure 4.5. Click the right arrow in this palette to see additional options. These options are applied in the same way as the options were applied in previous palettes, including the Brush palette from the Options bar.
9. To apply a style, double-click on it.

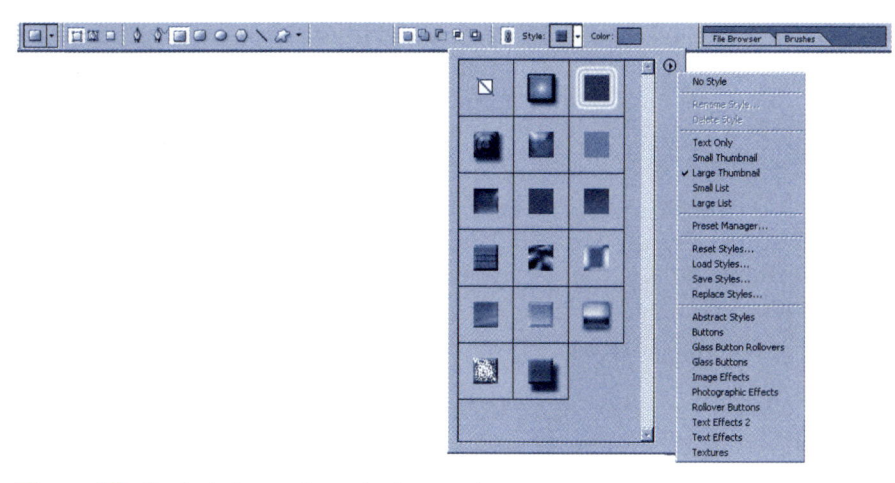

Figure 4.5 The Style button from the Options bar.

Click on the other arrows and options in the Options bar. You'll see options to change the default way a shape is drawn, among other things. It's best to leave the defaults the way they are for now though, at least until you get familiar with how the program works.

You'll use the other shapes similarly. To draw an ellipse for instance, choose the **Ellipse** tool. To create a polygon, choose the **Polygon** tool. After choosing a tool, check the Options bar for options. As an example, when the Polygon tool is chosen, there's an option for how many sides the polygon should have. That's an important attribute of the shape.

Use the **Line** tool to create lines, and lines with arrows on the ends of them. Drawing lines using the Lines tool creates an additional layer just like drawing any other shape does, and Photoshop really just thinks of this line as a rectangle. To draw lines, just click and drag. When the Line tool is chosen, there are options to configure the width of the line too, as well as the colour of the line itself and any arrowheads you add.

Finally, the **Custom Shapes** tool offers lots of shapes that can be added to your work that are already created. These include shapes like arrows, tickmarks, musical symbols, animals, frames, objects, ornaments, symbols and even speech bubbles.

To use the Custom Shapes tool:

1. Choose the **Custom Shapes** tool from the Toolbox. It is located with the other Shape tools.
2. From the Options bar, click on the down arrow next to the **Shape** box.

3. From the resulting palette, similar to that shown in Figure 4.5, click the right arrow to see the additional options.
4. Choose any other category to view the artwork available.
5. To select any custom shape, double-click on it, and then click and drag on the canvas.
6. The new shape will be filled with the style and/or the colour selected in the Options bar.

Adjusting the size

Once the shape is drawn, it is easily edited. In order to edit the shape, though, you have to select it.

To select a shape for editing:

1. Select **Window > Workspace > Reset Palette Locations**. You won't have to do this every time; this is just to make sure all of your palettes are in the right place!
2. Locate the **Layers** palette on the right side of the screen.
3. Click the **Layers** tab.
4. Locate the shape you want to edit in this palette and click on it. A thin, black line will be placed around the shape.

With the shape selected, edit the shape:

1. Select the **Move** tool from the Toolbox (it's the first one on the right-hand side).

If you don't want the new shape to be filled, configure the colour to be the same as the background colour in the Options bar.

2. Click, hold and drag on the shape to move it to another location on the screen.
3. Change the colour of the shape by double-clicking on the shape in the **Layers** palette and choosing a new colour from the **Color Picker** dialogue box that appears.
4. To apply a gradient to a shape, choose **Layer > Change Layer Content > Gradient**, or **Layer > Change Layer Content > Pattern** and set the options as desired.
5. Choose **Edit > Transform Path > Rotate** and use the cursor to rotate the image. Press **Enter** on the keyboard or click on the checkmark on the Options bar to accept, or press **Esc** on the keyboard or **Cancel** on the Options bar to cancel.

There are lots of other ways to edit the shape, and additional ways to rotate too. Start with a new canvas and place one rectangular shape on it. Then do the following:

1. Right-click on the shape and choose **Free Transform Path**.
2. Handles (also called control points) now surround the shape. Position the mouse outside this box, and when the cursor changes to a two-headed curved arrow, click and drag to rotate.
3. Click and drag on any handle to enlarge it by pulling outward, or make it smaller by pushing inward.
4. Click on any side handle to make it wider or taller.
5. Hold down the **Ctrl** key while dragging to freely transform and distort the shape into anything you want.
6. Right-click again on the shape to apply transformations such as Skew, Distort, Rotate, Scale and Perspective.

While there are lots of other ways to modify shapes, including using the Path Selection and Direct Selection tools from the Toolbox, it's beyond our level of knowledge at the moment. After working through Chapters 5, 6 and 7, and learning about paths and layers, come back to shapes and experiment with those tools.

Summary

In this chapter you were introduced to the most basic of art tools. The Pencil tool, the Brush tool, the Eraser tools and the Shape tools are all an important part of creating artwork from scratch. However, don't get stuck thinking that these tools can only be used for drawing and erasing – they can also be used to touch up blemishes in photographs, erase objects from images, and create photographic artwork.

Modifying paths

5

A quick refresher

Drawing with the Pen tool

Using the Path Selection tool

Using the Direct Selection tool

Rasterising paths

Summary

Vector graphics are mathematically defined and can be resized without losing their quality. Circles, for instance, are defined by how far the points on the outside of the circle are from the centre of it. Circles can thus be resized without distortion, because a new calculation is made for the new image. Bitmap (or raster) images use pixels to define how they look. Bitmap images lose quality and resolution when resized.

When thinking of paths, you probably conjure up some tree-lined, scenic, well-travelled country lane that you can follow to get from point A to point B. The path might be straight in some places and curved in others. Points on the path define the shape of it. Paths in Photoshop are similar, and are also defined by their points.

In this chapter you'll learn about paths and drawing them with the Pen tool, as well as using selection tools for working with the paths you create. There's the Path Selection tool for moving, merging, copying and deleting paths, and the Direct Selection tool for reshaping paths using their anchor points. You'll also learn about rasterising paths, which converts the vector paths into bitmap (raster) images.

A quick refresher

When drawing a shape with the Pen tool, you'll draw lines and curves to create it. These shapes are called paths. The lines and curves that make up the shape are called path segments. Paths can be open or closed. Closed paths are closed shapes such as circles, rectangles, squares, and so on – the shape you draw doesn't have to be one of these, however. Open paths have a start and end point, like a line or curve, and the ends do not meet.

Because paths are vector objects and contain no pixels, unless they are filled with colour they don't print out when you print your artwork. Paths consist of one or more lines or curved segments, and anchor points mark where the beginning and end of the lines and curves are. Anchor points also define curves and corners.

Drawing with the Pen tool

If you aren't quite clear about paths, segments, vector images and anchor points yet, follow along here to draw a few paths using the Pen tool, and hopefully it will become clearer.

To draw straight lines and shapes:

1. Open a new file using **New > File**, choose RGB colour, a white background and 1024 × 78.
2. Locate the **Pen** tool in the Toolbox; it is located ninth down on the left-hand side. You can also select the Pen tool by pressing **P** on the keyboard. From the Options bar, right-click on the Pen tool on the far left of the bar and choose **Reset Tool**. The Pen tool and Options bar are shown in Figure 5.1.
3. To draw a line, click the mouse twice on the canvas. A line will be drawn between the two points. The two square points at the beginning and end of the line are called anchor points.
4. Click on the **Pen** icon in the Toolbox to apply the line.
5. Click again on the canvas to draw a new line. Notice that the first line (path) disappears. This happens because the path (shape) was not closed, and was not filled with colour. Paths that are not defined by pixels or are not saved manually will not remain on the screen when a new path is created. This time, hold down the **Shift** key before clicking on the canvas a second time. Holding down the **Shift** key constrains the angle to a multiple of 45 degrees. A straight line is drawn.

Paths that are saved in an image are opened with the image the next time the file is opened.

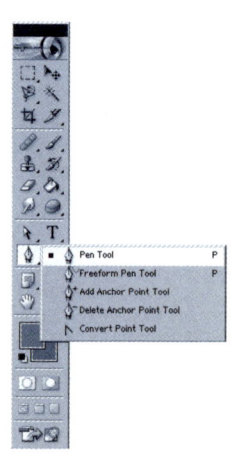

Figure 5.1 Locating the Pen tool.

6. Click again on the canvas, but do not hold down the **Shift** key. You should have a completed triangle at this time. Three points make up a triangle, and each connects to the other automatically. The inside of the triangle is filled with the foreground colour.
7. To save the new path (shape), click on the **Paths** tab of the **Layers** palette. Double-click on the path to save it. In the **Save Path** dialogue box, name the path '*Triangle*'. Click OK.

Take a look at the Options bar; it is shown in Figure 5.1. You'll see that all of the Shape tools are there. That's because the Shape tools also create paths when used, just like the Pen tools do. As with the Shape tools (which were introduced in the last chapter), there are additional ways to define how the shapes are drawn, including **Add to Shape Area**, **Subtract From Shape Area**, **Intersect Shape Areas** and **Exclude Overlapping Shape Areas**. There are also **Style** and **Color** options. For more information about these options, refer to Chapter 4.

The **New Shape Layer** button allows you to create a new layer when creating the shape. The icon beside it, **Paths**, enables you to create a new work path.

To draw curves shaped like semicircles (or the letter C) using the Pen tool, try this:

1. Using a new, blank canvas, select the **Pen** tool or hit the **P** key on the keyboard.
2. Position the cursor where you want the curve to begin. Click and hold down the mouse button.
3. Drag the mouse where you want the curve to be drawn; in this case, to the right. You'll see the pointer change to show one of two direction points. If you want the tool to move in multiple of 45 degrees, hold down the **Shift** key while dragging. Release the mouse button at the first direction point. Step 1 in Figure 5.2 shows this step. Click and drag to the right, the direction the curve should go.
4. Now, position the cursor where you want the curve to end, and drag in the opposite direction (left) to complete the curved segment. This is shown in Step 2 in Figure 5.2. Click and drag to the left, away from the direction of the curve.

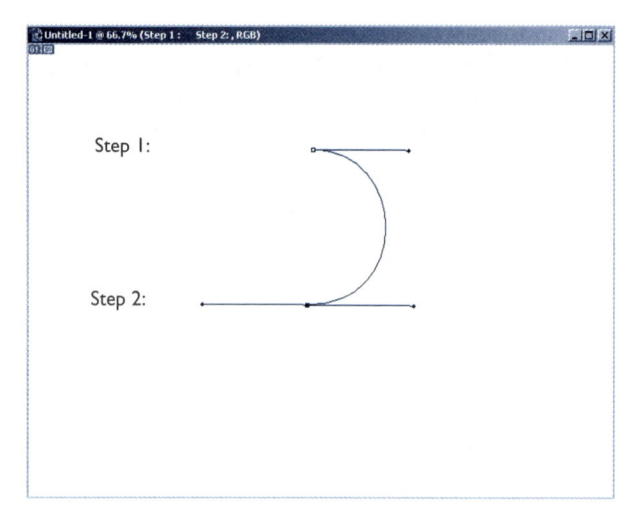

Figure 5.2 Drawing semicircles and curves.

5. Now, just click in various places on the canvas to add anchor points and curved segments.
6. If you want to turn this path into a closed shape, click the first point on the path. The icon will change from a pen to a pen with a small circle beside it.

To draw curves shaped like the letter S:

1. Position the cursor where you want the curve to begin. Click and hold down the mouse button.

2. Drag the mouse in the direction you want the curve to be drawn. You'll see the pointer change to show one of two direction points. If you want the tool to move in multiples of 45 degrees, hold down the **Shift** key while dragging. Release the mouse button at the first direction point. Step 1 in Figure 5.2 shows this step. Click and drag to the right, the direction the curve should go.
3. Now, position the cursor where you want the curve to end, and drag in the same direction as before to complete the curved segment. Click and drag to the left, away from the direction of the curve. Click the **Pen** tool to apply.
4. Continue experimenting with this tool until you can draw various shapes and lines. They don't have to be perfect though; in the next section you'll learn how to edit the paths you've drawn.

You can apply the Pen and Shape tools to create your own specific shapes and artwork, or to trace over an image in a photograph. These can then be saved in the Paths palette for later use.

Using the Path Selection tool

The **Path Selection** tool is located directly above the Pen tool. Click and hold on this icon (an arrow) to see the available selection tools and to select it. With this tool, you can click on any path to edit it. With the path selected, just click and drag to move it to another area of the screen.

You can use this tool in combination with other keys and the Options bar choices to perform many different editing tricks on paths. Here are just a few of them:

*The anchor points are the square points on a curve or line segment. Once the curve, line or shape is drawn, it can be edited by dragging these points around. You can add anchor points by clicking with the **Add Anchor Point** tool located in the choices with the Pen tool. See earlier in Figure 5.1. Anchor points can also be removed.*

- When the **Path Selection Tool** is chosen, the Options bar changes to offer additional options. Place a tick in the **Bounding Box** checkbox to place a bounding box around the path. Using this box, you can resize and rotate the path.
- Hold down the **Shift** key to select multiple segments.
- To merge overlapping path components, use the **Path Selection** tool, select the path from the **Paths** palette, and click the **Combine** button on the Options bar. All overlapping path components will be combined into one.
- To create duplicate copies of a path, hold down the **Alt** key while dragging.
- To delete a path component, select it and press the **Backspace** key on the keyboard.
- To align path components, hold down the **Shift** key while selecting the paths to align, then click one of the alignment tools in the Options bar. There are several, including **Align Top Edges**, **Align Vertical Centers**, **Align Bottom Edges**, **Align Vertical Edges**, and more.

With a little practice, you can learn how to trace or draw practically any object. These objects can be used for logos, for digitising images for embroidery, for creating vector reproductions of bitmap images, for designing original artwork, and so on.

Using the Direct Selection tool

The **Direct Selection** tool is located directly above the Pen tool. Click and hold on this icon (an arrow) to see the available selection tools and to select it. With this tool, you can click on any path to edit it.

As with the Path Selection Tool, there are several ways to use the Direct Selection Tool for editing vector images:

- To move a line segment, just click on it and drag.
- To reshape a curved segment, click on the curved segment to select it, click on one of the segments anchor points, and drag.
- To move multiple curved segments, use the **Shift** key and mouse to select them, then drag with the mouse to the new location.
- Delete a segment by selecting it then hitting the **Backspace** key.
- For closed paths, right-click on the path in the **Paths** palette and choose **Fill Path** to fill the closed shape with the foreground colour.
- To define a custom shape and save your creation, right-click on the shape and chose **Define Custom Shape**. Name the shape and it will be saved in the Custom Shape options.

Use the paths you created earlier to practise these techniques on. It is quite possible to create a circle using the Pen tool and change it completely using the anchor points and the Direct Selection tool.

Rasterising paths

A raster image is a bitmap image; it consists of pixels that define how it looks, what colour it is, what resolution and quality is configured, and so on. It is a common format for photographs and digital images, because of its ability to use colours effectively and produce quality images. Bitmap images are edited using their pixels, and because there is a fixed amount of pixels in an image, resizing the image can result in quality loss.

Photoshop 7

You cannot use painting tools or other options like filters on vector images. If you want to do this, you'll have to rasterise them first.

As you know already, paths, shapes and other objects drawn with the Pen tools are not raster images: they are vector images. These images are not edited using pixels; they are edited using their mathematical representations. In order to use vector images in the same manner as bitmap or raster images would be used, they must be 'rasterised' first.

Layers can be rasterised from the **Layer** menu or from the **Layers** and **Paths** palettes. Figures 5.3 and 5.4 show the menu choices for rasterising an image from the palettes.

To experiment with rasterising shapes and layers:

1. Open a new file and add some shapes and paths to it. Configure it as RGB. Use the Shape and Pen tools to create both open and closed shapes.
2. From the **Layers** palette, click the **Layers** tab. If it isn't on the workspace, choose **Window > Workspace > Reset Palette Locations**.

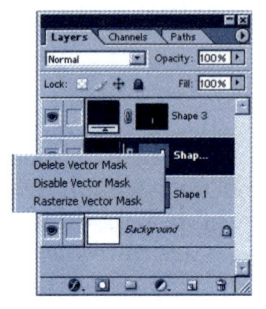

Figure 5.3 Rasterising a vector mask.

Figure 5.4 Rasterising a layer.

3. Right-click on the shapes and layers and choose **Rasterize Vector Mask** and/or **Rasterize Layer**, as shown in Figures 5.3 and 5.4.
4. Once rasterised, there will no longer be any paths in the Paths palette, and the shape will appear as a shape on a transparent layer.

You can also rasterise all layers using **Layer > Rasterize > All Layers**.

With the layers rasterised you can treat them as you would any other layers. But what are layers? In the next couple of chapters, we'll discuss that.

Summary

In this chapter you learned a little about paths. When using the Pen tool or the Shapes tool, paths are created. These can be saved and edited, and virtually any shape can be created. There are two selection tools for editing purposes, the Path Selection tool and the Direct Selection tool. Paths can be created for original artwork, or to trace around existing images.

Mastering layers   6

What is a layer?
Introducing the Layers palette
Creating and destroying layers
Showing and hiding layers
Locking and unlocking layers
Copying between layers
Linking layers
Grouping layers
Merging layers
Flattening the image
Summary

Throughout this book, I've made references to layers and the Layers palette. But what exactly is a layer, and why have I waited this long to talk about it?

To make learning easy initially, I had you open photos and other images and edit them using the more common tools in Photoshop. When working with images from a scanner or a camera, you worked on single-layer images. A single-layer image is an image with only one level of data, i.e. the image itself.

Multiple-layer images contain this first layer and others. Remember the picture of the birdhouse in Chapter 3? I cut the birdhouse out of one image and then pasted in on to another. The new image was the original photograph (one layer) and the birdhouse (the second layer). The birdhouse layer could then be edited independently of the image layer. The birdhouse was not in the original picture, and thus not in the same layer.

What is a layer?

Still don't get layers? Think about the overhead transparencies you may have seen used in meetings or presentations. Each transparency (a clear, plastic overlay, like an OHP slide) contains an image or data. One transparency can have a graph with titles printed out to the side, and another transparency can be laid on top of it that contains numbers that match up with the graph. As more transparencies are added, more 'layers' are added to what you view from the overhead. The same is true of Photoshop images. A picture can be one layer, text can be added as another layer, and so on.

Let's look at an image that contains multiple layers.

1. Open Photoshop 7.0 and choose **File > Open**.
2. You want to find the Samples folder. Click on the down arrow next to **Look In**. Locate the root drive (usually C:), click on **Program Files**, click on **Adobe**, then **Photoshop 7.0**. From here, click on the **Samples** folder.
3. From the Samples folder, open the file Flowers.psd.
4. Reset the palette locations by selecting **Window > Workspace > Reset Palette Locations**. Leave this file open for the next exercise.
5. Look at the Layers palette. Notice that there are five layers listed. This image was created from a background layer, which is a photograph, text was added creating a second layer, and then sunflowers were added, creating additional layers.

With this basic understanding of layers, let's focus for a minute on this palette.

Introducing the Layers palette

The Layers palette contains the information you'll need to manage and work with layers, and is shown in Figure 6.1.

From this palette, you can view all layers, layer effects, and how layers are grouped (if at all). You can also create, hide, display, copy, delete, view thumbnails, change opacity, configure blends, create adjustment layers, and so on. Familiarise yourself with this palette by hovering the mouse over each icon at the bottom of the palette. Click on the icons with arrows on them to see additional options. Right-click on the layer names in the palette to see additional options. Throughout this chapter, you'll learn how to use these options.

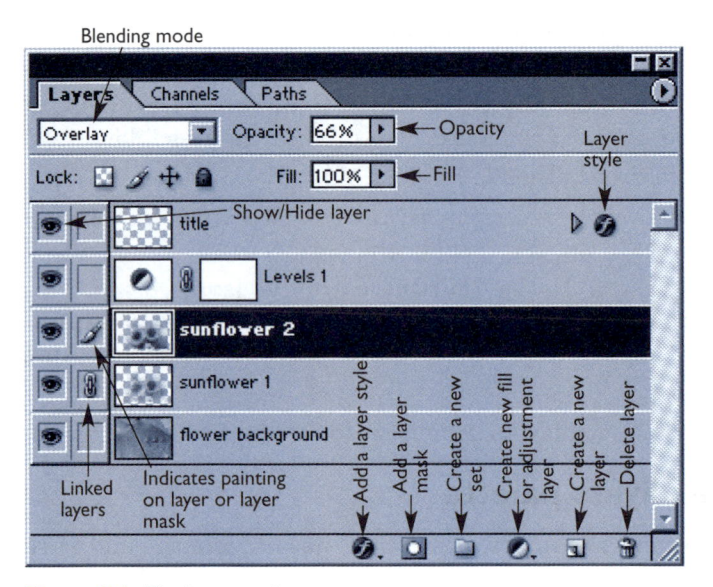

Figure 6.1 The Layers palette.

Continue these steps from the last exercise to manipulate a layer independently of the other layers in the image:

6. Look at the Layers palette under the Layers tab. There are five layers. Click once on the layer **Sunflower2**.
7. From the Toolbox, select the **Move** tool. It is the top right tool.
8. From the Options bar, place a tick in the box **Show Bounding Box**.

9. Notice the bounding box that now surrounds the sunflowers. Using the mouse, drag the sunflowers to another area of the image. The sunflowers are in a layer of their own and can thus be edited independently of the others.
10. Choose **File > Close**. When prompted to save changes, choose **No**.

What you've just experienced is how to edit a part of an image without disturbing the rest of it. This is an option only when you have layers in the image. This is impossible with single-layered images.

Creating and destroying layers

There are several ways to create a layer; for instance you can add text to the image as shown in the Flowers.psd file earlier. Adding text automatically creates a new layer. The text can then be edited without affecting the layers underneath it. You can add a shape to an image too, which automatically creates new layers. The same is true when drawing with the Pen tool.

Another way to add a layer involves pasting a selection on to an image, like the birdhouse we pasted to the image in Chapter 3. Pasting objects on to an image is fun too, especially if you are adding people to images where they shouldn't be.

From the Layer menu, you can add duplicate layers, apply a style to a layer, create adjustment layers, and group and link layers. Finally, you can add layers that are empty or contain a fill such as a colour, gradient or pattern. You'll learn about these in this chapter and the next.

When working with multi-layered images, you must select the layer you wish to work on from the Layers palette first.

Let's practise creating some layers:

1. Open a new file from **File > New**, and choose 1024 × 768, RGB, white background.
2. Reset the palettes if necessary using **Window > Workspace > Reset Palette Locations**.
3. Locate the Layers palette and the Layers tab. Add a shape using any **Shape** tool (see Chapter 4) and watch a new layer appear in this palette.
4. Add a line or shape with the **Pen** tool (see Chapter 5) and watch a new layer appear in this palette.
5. Add a new layer using **Layer > New > Layer**. In the **New Layer** dialogue box, type in a name for the layer, and click **OK**. Notice the new layer in the Layers palette. It has a chequered background because there is currently nothing on it.
6. Click on this new layer in the Layers palette, and use the **Paint Bucket** tool to fill the layer with the foreground colour. (The Paint Bucket tool was introduced in Chapter 3.)
7. Click on the new layer in the Layers palette. Locate the **Fill** option in this palette. Click on it and move the slider to the left, to about 50%, or type in 50%. Notice that the fill colour changes, but the layer's other attributes remain the same.
8. Click on the **Shape** layer in the Layers palette. Locate the **Opacity** option in this palette. Click on it and move the slider to the left, to about 50%, or type in 50%. Notice that the colour changes, but the layer's other attributes remain the same. Opacity determines how 'see-through' an object is.

9. Select a layer to delete in the Layers palette. Choose **Layer > Delete > Layer** to delete it. When prompted, choose **Yes** to delete.
10. Close this file without saving. Use **File > Close**.

With the basics of creating layers out of the way, let's open up another file from the Sample folder and practise with other layer options.

Showing and hiding layers

Besides adding and deleting layers, you can also show or hide them. Hiding a layer doesn't remove it, it just takes it out of view. Hidden layers aren't printed when the image is complete.

Open the file Morning Glass.psd from the Samples folder. Look at the Layers palette; there are 18 layers. Each layer contains something that is important to the picture. Follow this example to see how some of these layers can be shown or hidden:

1. With the file Morning Glass.psd open, locate the layer **boat_med** in the Layers palette.
2. Click on the eye next to the layer name in the Layers palette. The brown part of the boat disappears. Click it again to bring it back into view.
3. Click on the layer named **Layer 1** in the Layers palette. Hide and show that layer.
4. Don't close this just yet; we'll use it in the next section.

Hiding layers can be helpful when you want to keep a layer and its contents, but you need to work on other layers in the image without that particular layer getting in the way. By hiding finished layers, you can focus on what's left.

After copying an image or selection using **Edit > Copy**, *you can paste it on to an image using* **Edit > Paste** *to create a new layer. You can also use* **Layer > New > Layer Via Copy** *and* **Layer > New Layer Via Cut** *to copy and cut selections to new layers.*

Locking and unlocking layers

When you don't need to see the layer, hide it; if you need to see the layer but don't want to accidentally change it, lock it.

Locking a layer is helpful when you've completed the editing on a specific layer or part of a layer and don't want to accidentally change it when making other edits to the image. When a layer is locked, there is a lock icon showing in the Layers palette next to the locked layer(s).

There are several ways to lock layers and parts of layers. Figure 6.2 shows four options:

- **Lock Transparent Pixels** – locks the current opacity of a layer; you can't lighten or darken with any tools.
- **Lock Image Pixels** – locks out any painting tools; you can't paint on a layer with this locked.
- **Lock Position** – locks out any movement; you can't move a layer or object on it with this locked.
- **Lock All** – locks out everything; cumulative of previous three choices.

The first three choices partially lock a layer, and the last one fully locks it.

Locking a layer is easy:

1. Select the layer from the Layers palette.
2. Select the **Lock** option.
3. Notice that the lock icon is now shown next to the name of the layer in the Layers palette.

To see how this works, open the file Morning Glass.psd from the Samples folder, and fully lock a layer. Then, select the **Move** tool and try to move the layer. An error message will appear that says 'Could Not Complete The Request Because The Layer Is Locked'.

6: Mastering layers 119

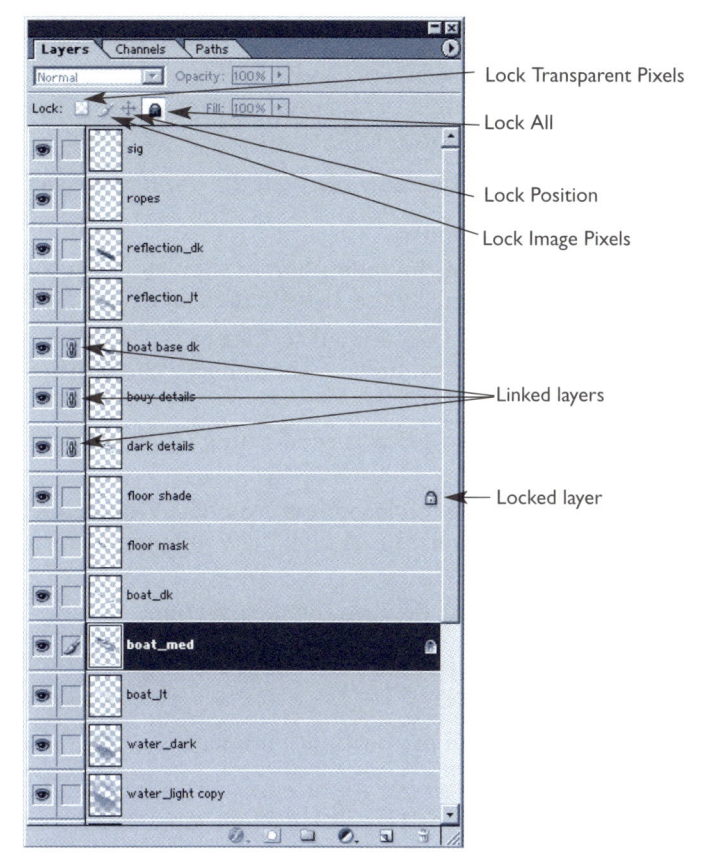

Figure 6.2 Locking layers using the Layers palette.

Copying between layers

Images can be copied between layers. These layers can be in the same image or they can be layers of different images. One way to move a selection from one image to another is to copy and paste it. However, there are other ways too.

To copy a layer within an image or to create a new file with the duplicate layer:

1. Select the layer to copy in the Layers palette.
2. Click **Layer > Duplicate Layer** from the menu bar or right-click on the layer to copy from the Layers palette and choose **Duplicate Layer**.
3. From the **Duplicate Layer** dialogue box, shown in Figure 6.3, type in a name for the layer or accept the default name, and then choose the destination for the layer.
   - If the destination is in the same file, in this case Morning Glass.psd, just click **OK**.
   - If it is to be a new layer in a new file, choose **New** from the **Document** window and type in a name for the new file. A new file will open, and the duplicate copy will be placed on it.
   - If it is to be a new layer for an existing file, see the next section.
4. Click **OK**.

To duplicate or copy layers between images:

1. Open both images, the source image and the destination image.
2. Select a layer from the Layers palette.
3. Drag the layer from the Layers palette to the destination image or choose **Layer > Duplicate Layer**. From the **Duplicate Layer** dialogue box, choose the open image from the **Document** window and click **OK**.

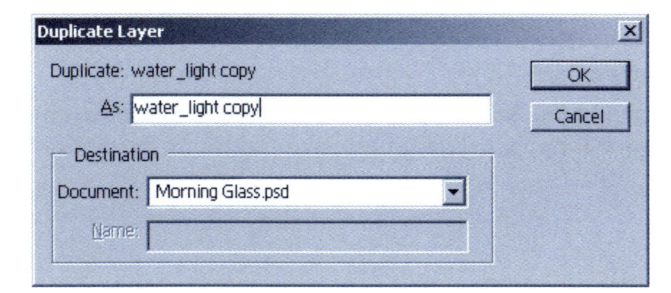

Figure 6.3 Duplicating layers.

Duplicating a layer is a great way to move entire selections to other images, or to duplicate a layer for editing when you aren't sure if you really want to apply changes to the layer in the image. By duplicating a layer in an image, you can edit it, and if it doesn't turn out the way you want, you can just delete it.

Linking layers

Once you've got several layers just the way you want them, you can link them so they can be moved together. Think about the Morning Glass.psd file, and how many layers it took to create the boat. If you need to move all of these layers together, you can link them and make them act like a single object instead of 12 or 15 separate ones.

The linked layers, now acting as a single layer, can be copied, pasted, moved, transformed and otherwise manipulated just as single-layer images can. This allows you to use multiple layers to create an object, and then group them to manipulate as a single one.

So far, we've been talking about layers and not layer sets. You might have noticed that Layer Set is also an option when choosing to duplicate or otherwise edit a layer. Layer sets are special kinds of layers that you can create to hold other layers. It's a bit like linking layers, detailed in the next section. There will be more about creating a layer set later in the section on grouping layers.

If you are having trouble locating where to click to link, see Figure 6.2. There is a link icon and a callout for that figure.

You can always rename layers or layer sets from the Layers palette by double-clicking on the name and typing in a new one.

To link layers:

1. Select a layer in the Layers palette.
2. Click in the Layers palette to the left of any layers you want to link to the selected layer. A link icon will appear. The linked layers can now be worked with as a single entity.

Grouping layers

Layers can also be grouped together. When layers are grouped as a **layer set**, the layer can be locked, the layers in the set can be moved as a group, transformations and other effects can be applied to all of the layers in the layer set, and you can reduce the number of entries in the Layers palette.

To group layers and create a layer set:

1. Click the **Create New Set** button in the Layers palette. This was shown in Figure 6.1 earlier. You can also choose **Layer > New > Layer Set** to create the new layer set. I prefer the latter because there is an option to name the layer set before creating it. The **New Set Button** in the Layers palette just names them Set 1, Set 2, etc.
2. A new folder will appear in the Layers palette. If you want to, set any layer options such as opacity or blending mode before continuing.
3. In the Layers palette, click and drag the layers from the Layers palette to the new folder to add them to the new layer set.

Now, you can apply changes to the entire set, including locking it.

Merging layers

When you are nearing the end of a project that has multiple layers, you can merge the finished layers to create partial versions of your completed image. Doing so not only helps you organise your thoughts and simplify the image, but also reduces the file size. File size is relative to the number of layers you have; the more layers, the larger the file.

To merge two layers or layer sets:

1. Open the Layers palette.
2. The layers you'll merge must be next to each other in this palette. If they are not, move one next to the other by dragging it from its location in the Layers palette to its new location next to the layer to merge to.
3. With the two layers positioned in the palette, one on top of the other, choose the layer that is the top item of the pair. Make sure both layers are visible and that they are not locked.
4. If the top item is a layer choose **Layer > Merge Down**. If the top item is a layer set, choose **Layer > Merge Layer Set**.

You can also merge other types of layers. For instance, from the **Layer > Merge Linked** command, all visible linked layers can be merged. To merge all of the visible layers and layer sets in an image, choose **Layer > Merge Visible**.

If you don't see Merge Down or Merge Layer Set in the Layers menu, make sure that they are not locked.

Flattening the image

When an image is flattened, all of the visible layers are merged together, and this includes the background layer. You shouldn't flatten a file until you are finished with it. Flattening greatly reduces file size, discards all hidden layers, and fills any transparent parts of the image with white.

To flatten a finished image:

1. Make sure all of the layers in the image are visible. Use the Layers palette to make sure none are hidden. Visible layers have an eye icon next to them; hidden layers do not.
2. Choose **Layer > Flatten Image**.

Summary

In this chapter you learned the basics of using layers, including using the Layers palette, creating and deleting layers, showing and hiding layers, locking and unlocking layers, copying between layers, linking, grouping and merging layers, and finally flattening layers. When working with nearly complete images, use the group and merge layers to reduce the file's size; for completed images, flatten the layers to greatly reduce the file's size.

Using layer commands

7

Creating fill layers
Creating adjustment layers
Aligning, arranging and distributing
Adding layer styles
Applying shadows and glows
Bevelling and embossing
Changing the global light
Creating layer masks
Working with blending modes
Summary

A gradient is a pattern of colours that fade into one another based on specific rules. Linear gradients blend and fade in lines; radial gradients blend and fade in circles; angle gradients blend by a specified angle diamond gradients blend in a diamond shape; and reflected gradients are symmetric linear gradients.

Now that you know a little about layers and creating and using them, let's talk about some special kinds of layers. In this chapter you'll learn about Fill layers, including solid, gradient and pattern layers, adjustment layers, and layer styles, including the styles shadows, glows and bevels. Layer masks will also be covered. These new layers and styles can be used to enhance your images, add effect, create Web designs, and much more.

Creating fill layers

Of the special layers available, **fill layers** are the easiest to use and configure. Fill layers can be created to serve as a background or effect-type layer that is a solid colour, a gradient, or a pattern. Once a fill is chosen, the Color, Mode and Opacity settings can be changed to blend in the new layer with the other layers in the image.

In the following example, we'll create different backgrounds using a fill layer, and experiment with the options available.

1. Select **File > New**, choose 1024 × 768, RGB colour, and white background.
2. Reset the palette locations from **Window > Workspace > Reset Palette Locations**.
3. Select **Layer > New Fill Layer > Solid Color**. Click **OK**.
4. From the Color Picker, choose a solid colour for this layer. Click **OK**.
5. From the **Edit** menu, choose **Undo New Color Fill Layer**.
6. Select **Layer > New Fill Layer > Gradient**. Click **OK** in the New Layer dialogue box.

7. From the Gradient Fill Dialogue box shown in Figure 7.1, click the down arrow next to the **Gradient** window. In the drop-down list, click the right arrow to see the additional options.

8. From this additional list, choose **Color Harmonies 1**, and click on **OK** when prompted to replace current gradients. Repeat this step with the other gradient types in this list. After exploring the various gradients, choose one from the **Noise Samples** group by clicking on it once. (Do not press OK in the Gradient Fill dialogue box yet.)

9. The gradients in the Noise Levels group are all linear gradients; they are configured by lines. You can see the new gradient in the file in Photoshop as it is chosen, as shown in Figure 7.1.

10. From the Gradient Fill dialogue box, change the **Style** from **Linear** to **Radial** from the drop-down list. Try **Angle**, **Reflected** and **Diamond** too. As you choose each, change the angle by typing in a new number or dragging the angle manually from the **Angle** icon in the dialogue box. Choose **Radial** and change the **Scale** from 100% to 50% to make the radial design smaller or larger. Click **Reverse** to reverse the colours, select **Dither** to reduce banding, and deselect **Align with Layer** if you don't want the bounding box of the layer to be involved with applying the gradient.

11. Click **OK** when finished.

Creating a **pattern layer** is the same as creating a fill layer. To create a pattern layer, just select **Layer > New Fill Layer > Pattern** and use the Pattern Fill dialogue box in the same manner as you used the Fill Layer dialogue box. This technique only adds a layer to a new file. To add a fill layer to an existing image for effect, you'll have to change the opacity and fill of the layer so the existing layers will show though.

Photoshop 7

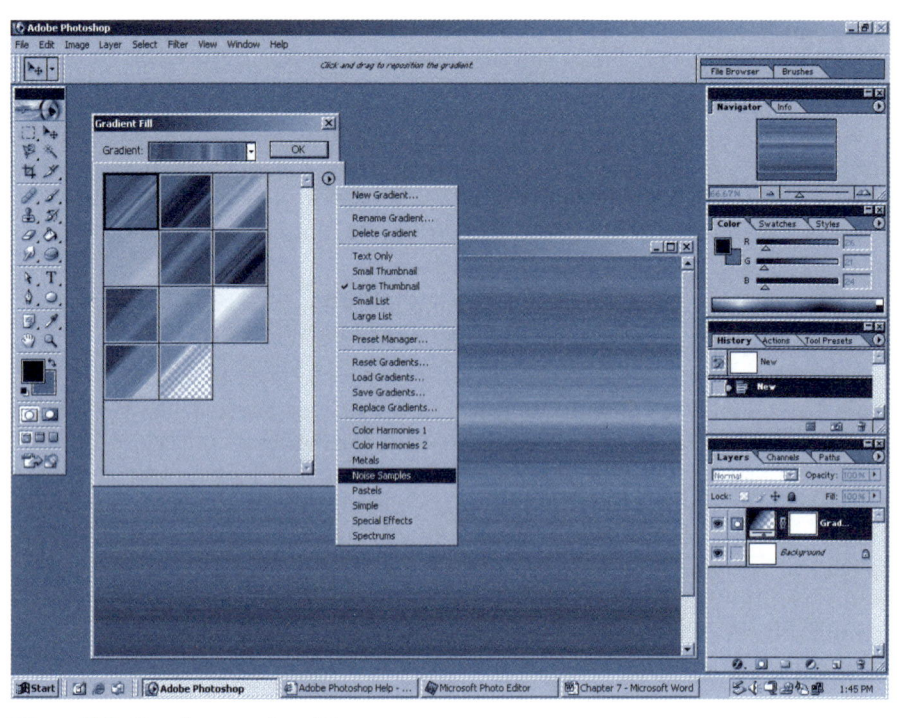

Figure 7.1 Creating a gradient fill.

Figure 7.2 shows a business card design with three layers: the text layer, which also contains the clip art, the white background layer, and the gradient layer. The fill of the gradient layer has been set at 46% so that the text layer can be seen. The opacity has been changed to 80% in order to lighten the gradient. The blending mode has been changed from Normal to Darken, so that the text and clip art will stand out. You'll learn about blending modes towards the end of this chapter, and text in the next chapter. Perhaps you can come back to this and create your own business card.

Creating adjustment layers

Adjustment layers allow you to experiment with adjustments to an image without making permanent changes to the image itself. In doing so, you can experiment to your heart's content without having to worry about permanently altering pixels in your image. The changes you make are applied to the adjustment layer only, and this layer acts as a sort of covering or transparent film over the actual image. The adjustment layer, since it resides on top of the other layers, affects all of the layers underneath it, which means you can make lots of changes while only using a single layer, eliminating the need to edit multiple layers separately. In addition, the adjustment layer can simply be deleted if desired.

To create an adjustment layer, click on the **New Adjustment Layer** button at the bottom of the Layers palette or click **Layer > New Adjustment Layer** and then choose an option from the menu choices. There are lots of choices.

From the choices, choose the option that most closely resembles the effect you'd like to have on the image (see the bulleted list next). Click **OK** to create the layer, and then configure the options.

Figure 7.2 A business card design with three layers.

Although there are several different types of adjustment layers to choose from, the choices I think you'll be most interested in initially are listed next, with a brief description of each and what can be configured.

- **Levels** – use this option to correct the colour balance of an image when shadows, highlights and midtones need adjusting. Use the sliders to make changes.
- **Color Balance** – use this option for general colour correction. There are sliders available for all of the colours that are used to make up the image.
- **Brightness/Contrast** – use this option when the image or object in the image is too dark or light, or doesn't stand out enough.
- **Hue/Saturation** – use this option to choose what colours to edit in the image. Sliders allow you to change any colour in the image.
- **Selective Color** – use this option to choose a colour to change, such as cyan, magenta, yellow or black in a CMYK image, or red, green or blue in an RGB image. Sliders enable you to change the selected colour only.
- **Gradient Map** – use this option to specify a gradient and set gradient options.
- **Invert** – use this to invert all of the colours in the image to create a negative effect. There are no options or sliders for this command.
- **Threshold** – use this to convert greyscale or colour images to black and white images. These image are high-contrast images and are more for special effects than for creating black and white images from colour ones. Move the sliders to increase or decrease contrast.

*When configuring the adjustment layer, you can see the changes as they are applied to the original image as long as the **Preview** box is selected.*

Aligning, arranging and distributing

Now that you've created all of these layers, how are you going to manage them? There are several options, and in this section I'll talk about aligning, arranging and distributing the layers.

Aligning layers

Aligning layers is one way to get the layers in the correct place in the image. You can align layers using the Move tool or you can align the layers using commands from the Layer menu on the menu bar. When the Move tool is selected, the Options bar changes to offer lots of alignment choices. You can hover the mouse over them to see each choice.

You can also align layers using **Layer > Align To Selection** or **Layer > Align Linked**. In both cases, from the Options bar or from this choice, there are six alignment choices:

- **Top Edges**
- **Vertical Centers**
- **Vertical Edges**
- **Left Edges**
- **Horizontal Centers**
- **Right Edges**.

In order to see the choices for alignment in the Options bar or from the Layer menu, multiple layers must be linked together for alignment.

To align layers in an image using the Move tool (using the Layer menu is similar):

1. Open a multi-layered image (such as the Flowers.psd file from the Samples folder).
2. You can align the layer to a selection in the image, to a selection border, or to the active layer. For aligning to a selection, use one of the selection tools to select the part of the image to use as the alignment guide. For aligning to the active layer, choose the active layer in the **Layers** palette.
3. With the selection or layer chosen to align *to*, choose the layers to align from the Layers palette and link them together. Linking layers was covered in Chapter 6.
4. Select the **Move** tool.
5. From the Options bar, choose one of the alignment options as listed earlier.

You can also use the Layer options to align layers.

Arranging layers
Arranging layers enables you to specify what will be in front and what will be at the back of an image. You can see how the layers are arranged in an image from the Layers palette, and you can change the order of them there by dragging them towards the top of bottom of the palette. You can also change the order of the layers using **Layer > Arrange**.

Look back at Figure 7.2. The order of the layers from bottom to top is the background layer, the text layer and the gradient layer. The gradient layer is on top. Compare what you see in Figure 7.2 with what is shown in Figure 7.3. In this figure, the text has been moved to the top-most position, meaning it is on top of the other layers. You can see why this is problematic.

Figure 7.3 Moving layers in the Layers palette.

Arranging layers enables you to add multiple layers or images and blend them in to one image. In Figures 7.2 and 7.3 the white image was scanned in to this file, and stands out. By adding a gradient layer, placing that layer on top of the others, and then working with opacity and fill, the white scanned part of the picture becomes unnoticeable.

To arrange layers, drag the layers from one area of the Layers palette to another, or use the **Layer > Arrange** command to move a layer backward or forward.

Distributing layers
Distributing layers is like aligning layers, and it allows you to organise the layers in an image. To distribute layers in an image, simply link three or more layers, select the **Move** tool, and choose a distributing type. The available distribution types are available from the Options bar when the Move tool is selected, and they are located next to the Alignment options. They are:

- **Distribute Top Edges**
- **Distribute Vertical Centers**
- **Distribute Vertical Edges**
- **Distribute Left Edges**
- **Distribute Horizontal Centers**
- **Distribute Right Edges**.

Layer styles cannot be applied to a background layer, a locked layer or a layer set.

Adding layer styles

Layer styles are effects that are applied to entire layers. These styles are linked to the layer and quickly change the look of it. There are lots of layer styles, including shadows, glows, bevels, and others. Using styles allows you to add emphasis to text, add shadows and glows to images, add texture to a layer, and create buttons to be used on websites. There are even styles to change the global lighting of a photograph.

Before we get started, open the Styles palette so that all of the styles are available.

1. Select **Window > Styles** from the menu bar. The Styles palette will appear as shown in Figure 7.4.
2. Drag the **Styles** tab from the Color palette to the centre of the workspace to form a separate palatte.
3. Click and drag on the bottom right corner of the Styles palette so that all of the default styles show. Click the right arrow in the drop-down list to see additional options. In Figure 7.4, **Large List** has been is chosen and the default styles are showing.
4. From this additional drop-down list, choose **Abstract Styles** and click **OK** to load them. View the available styles.
5. Repeat step 4 and choose **Buttons**.
6. Continue repeating these steps to see all of the available styles. After you've viewed them, choose **Reset Styles** from this list to revert back to the original style offerings.

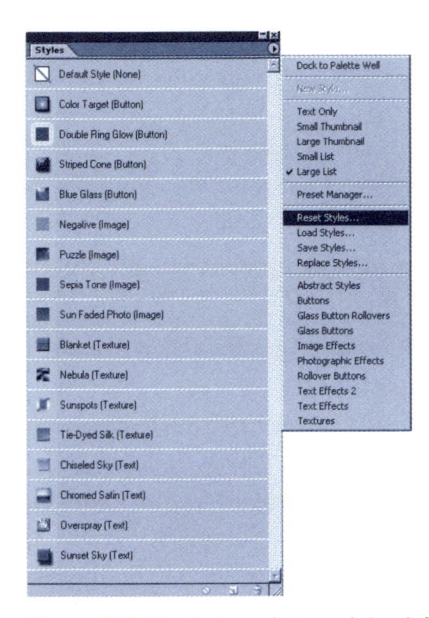

Figure 7.4 The Styles palette and the default styles.

You can also access **Layer Styles** from the **Layer** menu. **Choose Layer > Layer Style** and choose one of the options. There are several preset options and choosing one will open a dialogue box for configuration and customisation of the style. This is a fast and easy way to apply styles to an image without going through the Styles palette. The options under **Layer > Layer Style** are as follows:

- **Drop Shadow** – adds a shadow behind the layer contents.
- **Inner Shadow** – adds a shadow inside the layer, giving it a lower-level or recessed look.
- **Outer Glow** – adds a glow from the outside edges of a layer.
- **Inner Glow** – adds a glow from the inside edges of a layer.
- **Bevel and Emboss** – adds shadows and highlights to the layer.
- **Satin** – adds shading to the inside of the layer making it have a smooth finish.
- **Color Overlay** – superimposes a chosen colour.
- **Gradient Overlay** – superimposes a chosen gradient.
- **Pattern Overlay** – superimposes a chosen pattern.
- **Stroke** – outlines an object on the layer using a specific fill, such as colour, gradient or pattern.

While either technique (using the Styles palette or using the Layer menu) can be used to apply a style, I would recommend the **Layer > Layer Style** option for beginners. Just choose the type of style you want from the menu choices, and edit it from the dialogue box that appears. If you choose a style from the Styles palette and apply it by dragging it to the layer, the dialogue box won't show automatically. To see the dialogue box requires another step (clicking on the **Style** icon in the Layers palette). There will be more on all of this next.

Applying shadows and glows

With the Styles palette open and the default styles available as shown in Figure 7.4, notice that there are different types of styles available. There are styles for text, for images and for buttons. In the default list there is a single glow style named **Double Ring Glow (Button)**, but there are no shadows styles.

As you learned in the previous section, there are lots of other categories of styles. In several of them, you can find other glows and locate the shadow styles.

To apply an effect to an image using the Styles palette (in this case a shadow effect), perform these steps:

1. Drag the Styles palette out of the workspace area or back to the Color palette.
2. Open a file or image you would like to add a shadow to; perhaps a picture or a boat, or a logo you've created.
3. From the Styles palette, locate the style you want to apply. You can choose from any of them, but for this exercise use a style that has the word 'shadow' in it. The style **Inner Shadow** is available under the **Photographic Effects** choice; choose this one for this exercise.
4. Verify that the layer you want to add the style to is chosen in the Layers palette, and drag the style to the image to apply it. Depending on the style chosen, you may or may not see much of an effect immediately; that's OK, you can edit the style applied.
5. Locate the new style in the Layers palette. There will be two cursive fs in the Layers palette, one on the layer itself and one for the Inner Shadow style effect. Choose the one located with the Inner Shadow style effect. See Figure 7.5 to view the Layers palette and the Layer Style dialogue box, as well as the work area.

*If you aren't seeing these styles, click on the right arrow and choose **Reset Styles**. It's highlighted in Figure 7.4. You can also choose **Append** in the dialogue box to add the styles to your existing list instead of replacing it.*

*When applying multiple styles to an image, dragging the style over will replace the other styles applied by default. If you want to add this style to the old style with this new one, hold down the **Shift** key while dragging.*

6. The dialogue box you'll see if you chose Inner Style in step 3 is the same dialogue box you'd see if you chose **Layer > Layer Style > Inner Style**, without the extra step of opening it from the Layers palette. Use this dialogue box to configure how you want the image to look.

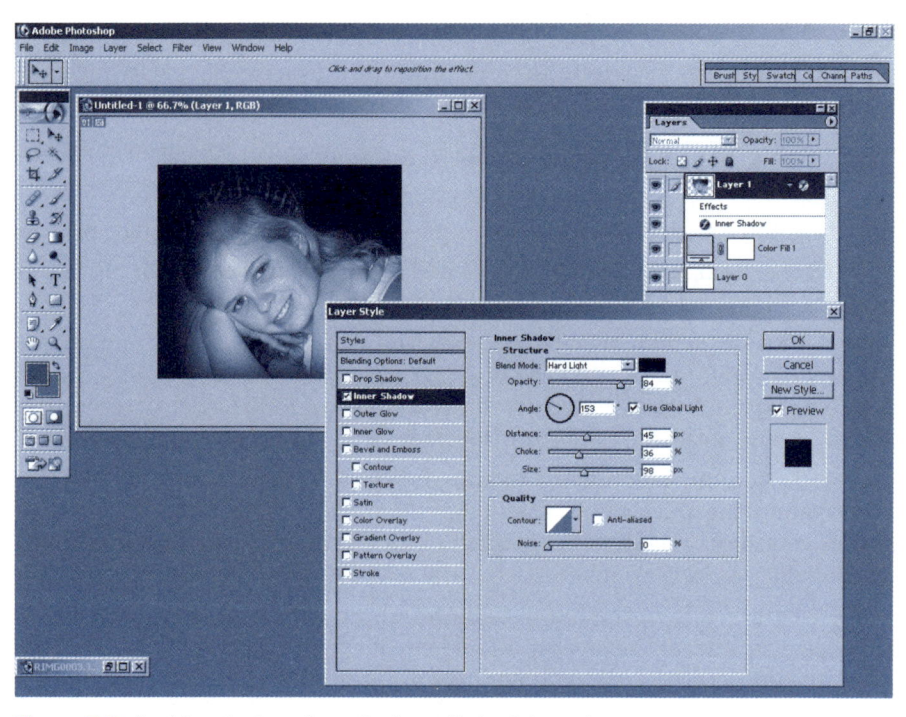

Figure 7.5 Applying shadows from the Layer Style dialogue box.

The best way to learn what each of these options are is to use them. The changes you make are applied immediately, as long as the **Preview** box is selected. Terms are fairly self-explanatory; for instance, **Distance** specifies the distance of the effect from the edges, **Angle** changes the angle of the effect **Choke** shrinks the boundaries of the effect and **Noise** adds distortion to the effect. Each layer style has different options, though, and not all can be applied to every one.

Glows are applied in the same manner as shadows, and can be used to add a 'halo' type of effect around an image or on a layer. The options in the Layer Styles dialogue box for a glow effect are different from shadow options. Some of them include the option to choose a gradient to apply for the glow, the technique to apply (softer or harder edges), the source (from where the glow should emanate), and jitter (varies colour and opacity), to name a few.

Bevelling and embossing

Bevelling and embossing can be used to create buttons for websites, or to add combinations of shadows and highlights to selected layers in an image. You've probably seen this effect used on the Internet and websites, or on signs for businesses. Using the **Bevel** and **Emboss** layer styles is performed the same as detailed earlier; just select an appropriate style from the Styles palette and drag it to the image, or choose **Layer > Layer Style > Bevel and Emboss**.

Figure 7.6 shows a Web icon for sending e-mail to a company. It was created by adding a shape to a new file, adding some text and lettering, and then by adding a bevel effect to the shape itself. The background was coloured blue using the Paint Bucket tool.

*Choose the style closest to the one to apply, experiment with the options in the Layer Styles dialogue box, and click **OK** when the desired result is established.*

Remember, if you drag from the Styles palette, you'll have to click on the cursive f in the Layers palette to see the dialogue box for editing that style; if you choose from the Layer menu, the dialogue box will appear automatically.

Figure 7.6 Using bevels to create Web buttons.

Changing the global light

If you've ever taken a picture and had it come out too dark, or if the image didn't have the correct lighting, you can change it using the **Global Light** style options. This style allows you to apply light to an image in order to add the light that's missing.

To set a global lighting angle for all of the layers in an image (which is normally what you'll want to do with photographs):

1. Open the photo that needs global light added to it.
2. Choose **Layer > Layer Style > Global Light**.
3. From the Global Light dialogue box, drag the angle to configure from where the light is shining, and click **OK**.

Figure 7.7 shows the Web button from Figure 7.6, with global light applied. The light is angled from the top left corner and shines light down on the button. This same technique can be applied to photos and other images.

If Layer Style is greyed out, double-click on the layer in the Layers palette and change it into a 'Normal' layer. These styles can't be applied to images with backgrounds only.

Creating layer masks

Layer masks are used to manage areas within a layer or layer set, and to control how selected parts of images will be shown or hidden. Layer masks are generally used to hide layers or parts of layers. Masks do not change the layer, only how it looks by masking parts of it. If you like the effect, you can keep it; if not, the layer mask can be discarded.

Layer masks can be created using the painting tools or the selection tools. To add a mask to hide or reveal a layer using the selection tools:

Before leaving this section, note that you can save a new style and use it as a preset. Just create the style by editing an existing one or combining several, choose **New Style** from the Style palette, and type in a name for the newly created style. You can also select the **New Style** button in the Layer Styles dialogue box when configuring a style to save it.

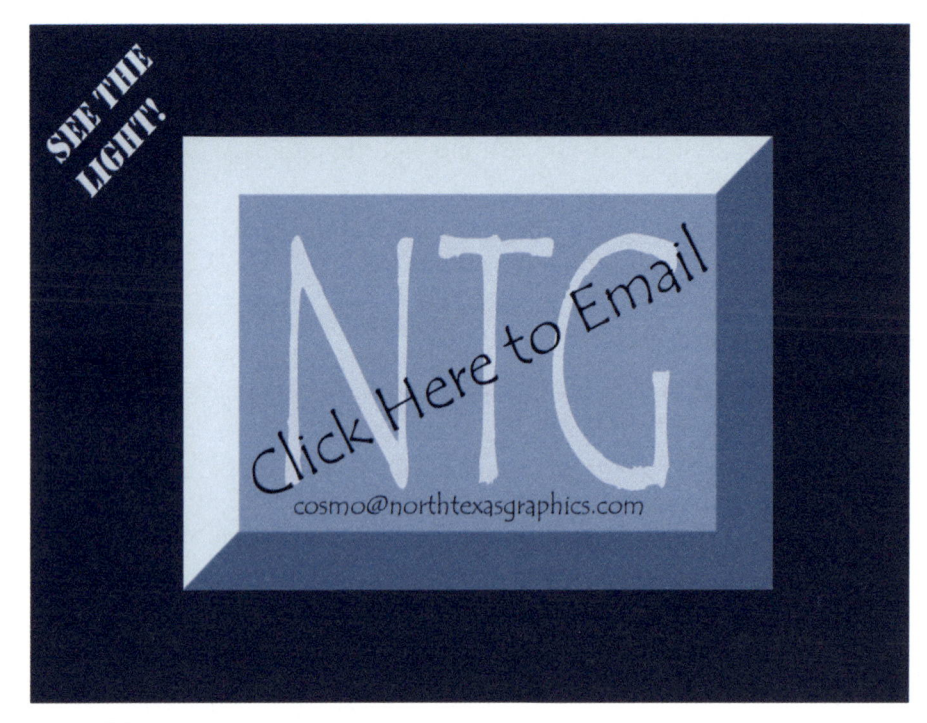

Figure 7.7 Global light applied to a Web button.

1. Make sure no parts of the image are selected.
2. Select the layer or layer set to mask (hide or show) in the Layers palette.
3. To show an entire layer, choose **Layer > Add Layer Mask > Reveal All**; to hide the entire layer, choose **Layer > Add Layer Mask > Hide All**.
4. Click on the **Layer Mask** thumbnail in the Layers palette. This activates the mask.
5. Select any painting tool or editing tool (see Chapters 3 and 4). Configure the Options bar with a brush big enough to paint over the parts of the layer to mask. If you want to mask the selection or layer only subtly, change the opacity from 100% to something less.
6. The foreground and background colours change to greyscale once the mask is activated. Paint using white, grey or black, and use the tool selected to paint on to the image or layer selection. Using white will reveal the layer, grey will make it partially visible, and black will hide it. You can switch between white and black by switching the foreground and background colours in the Toolbox.
7. The mask can be disabled and otherwise edited from the Layers palette. To see these options, right-click on the mask and choose from the drop-down list.

Working with blending modes

Finally, blending modes can be applied to layers to add additional effect. Blending modes are used to determine how the selected layer will blend in with the other layers in the image. There are far too many blending modes to go over in depth here, but a brief description of each is certainly in order.

The best way to understand blending modes is to view and apply them while reading through the different types described next. To view and apply the blending modes, open a file with at least two layers, and open the Layers palette. Double-click on a layer to open in the Layer Style dialogue box, which contains the blending options. (You can also right-click on the layer in the Layers palette and choose **Blending Options**.)

The Layer Style dialogue box is shown in Figure 7.8 with the blending options selected.

As you can see from Figure 7.8, there are several options for distributing the new pixels you are blending in with the other layers:

- **Normal** – the default mode for painting and the standard mode for a layer. Normal mode replaces the underlying pixels with the ones you've added.
- **Dissolve** – randomly distributes the pixels added and creates a textured look.
- **Darken** – changes only pixels that are lighter than the foreground colour.
- **Multiply** – darkens the image by decreasing the brightness, creating a shadow or charcoal effect.
- **Color Burn** – increases the contrast of the lowest layer of the image.
- **Linear Burn** – darkens the lower layer of the image.
- **Lighten** – changes only pixels that are darker than the foreground colour.
- **Screen** – lightens the image and gives it a faded look.
- **Color Dodge** – decreases the contrast by brightening the base colour of the image.
- **Linear Dodge** – increases brightness by increasing the base colour.

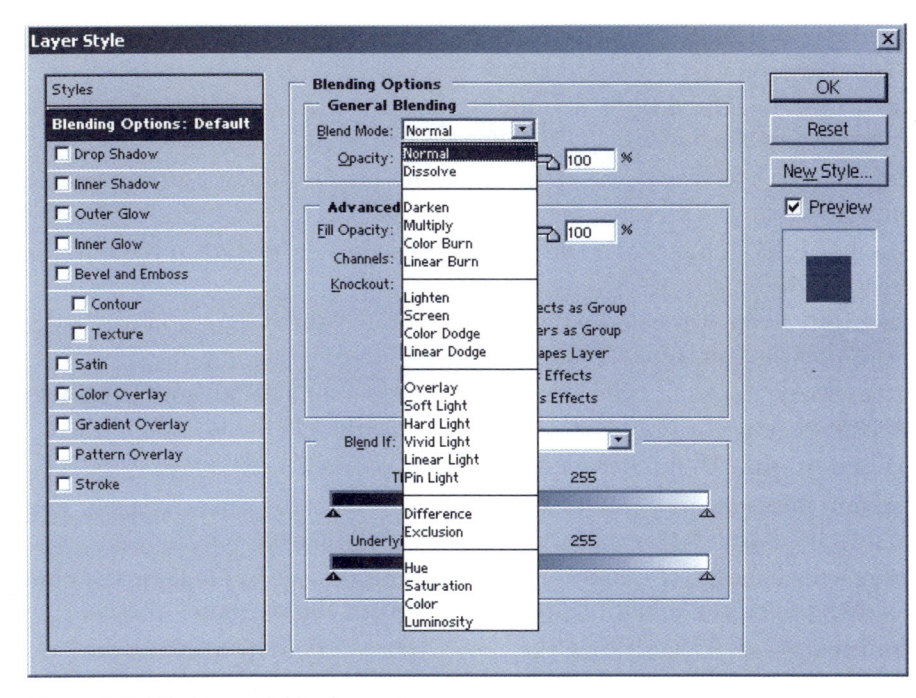

Figure 7.8 Working with blending options.

- **Overlay** – blends the majority of the new colours into the background, creating a ghosting or transparent effect.
- **Soft Light** and **Hard light** – softens or hardens the brightness of the image determined by the base colour. The effect is like shining a light on the layer.
- **Vivid Light** – changes the contrast of the pixels similar to the burn or dodge effects.
- **Linear Light** – changes the brightness of the pixels similar to the burn or dodge effects.
- **Pin Light** – replaces colours depending on the blend colour, and can make the new pixels look transparent.
- **Difference** – looks at the base colour and the blend colour and subtracts the darkest from the brightest. Gives a special effect to the layer.
- **Exclusion** – like Difference, but with lower contrast.
- **Hue** and **Saturation** – creates a new colour by blending the base colour and the blend colour and takes into account the attributes of each.
- **Color** – the opposite of Luminosity, creates a new colour by blending the base colour and the blend colour and takes into account the attributes of each.
- **Luminosity** – the opposite of Color, creates a new colour by blending the base colour and the blend colour and takes into account the attributes of each.

To apply a blend, simply configure it from the Layer Style dialogue box using the available sliders and options, and click **OK**.

Summary

In this chapter you learned some advanced layer commands such as creating fill layers, adjustment layers, and how to align, distribute and arrange layers. You also learned to apply layer styles, create layer masks and work with blending modes.

Adding type 8

Using the Type tool
Comparing Point Type and Paragraph Type
Adjusting type properties
The Character and Paragraph palettes
Other type options
Warping type
Rasterising type
Summary

Type (text) can be added to a file or image using the **Type** tool. The Type tool is located in the Toolbox and is the eighth one down the right-hand side as shown in Figure 8.1. There are four options: the Horizontal Type tool, the Vertical Type tool, the Horizontal Type Mask tool and the Vertical Type Mask tool. In this chapter, the focus will be on the first two.

Adding text to a file is easy: just choose the Type tool, click on the image and begin typing. Once the text is added, you can adjust the text's properties, including font, colour and size. You can also warp or rasterise the text. To begin, let's start with adding some text to an image.

Using the Type tool

Adding text to a file or image is one of the easiest ways to 'finish off' a project. You can add text to create a flyer, sales form, sign or logo, or even add a text balloon over the head of someone in a photo. Sometimes, text is just what you need to get your point across.

The Horizontal Type tool adds text to the image horizontally, and the Vertical Type tool adds text to the image vertically.

To add text to an image:

1. Click and hold the **Type** tool in the Toolbox – it's the eighth one down the right side. From the menu options, choose the **Horizontal Type** tool.
2. Click on the file you are working with where you'd like the text to begin.
3. In the Layers palette, a new text layer is created. From the Options bar shown in Figure 8.1, you can make choices for the size of the text, the font and other options.
4. Type in the text you want to add, or at least the first few words. Highlight them with the mouse. The words 'Using the Type tool' are highlighted in Figure 8.1.

8: Adding type 153

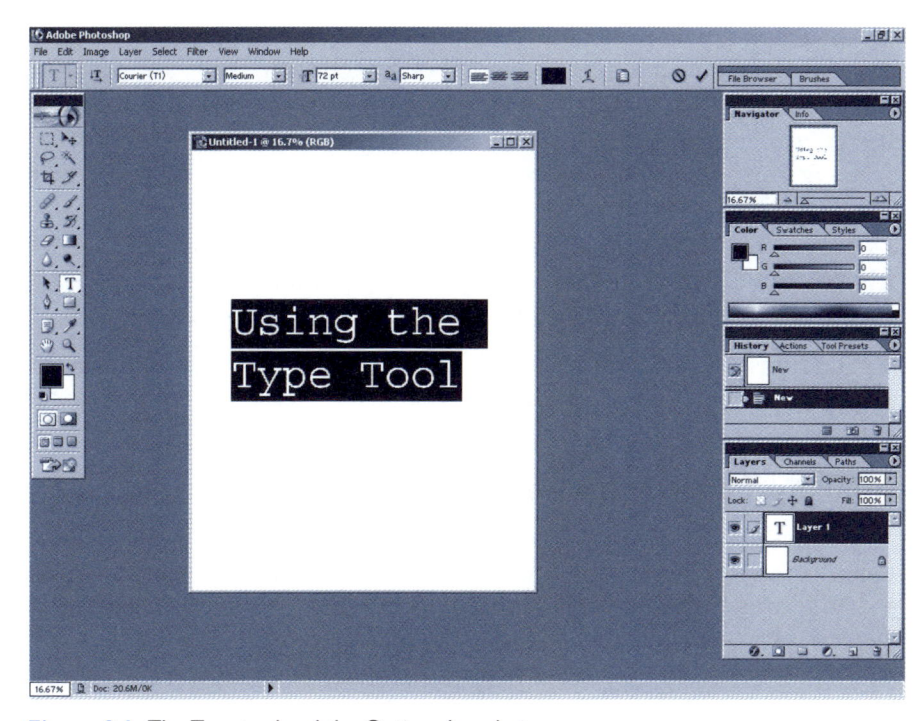

Figure 8.1 The Type tool and the Options bar choices.

5. From the Options bar, click the down arrow by the size window, and choose a size from the choices, or type in a size in the window by typing over the size indicated. Choose a size that fits your project.

If you try to recreate Figure 8.1, and incorporate the Pencil tool with a text layer as I've done, you'll be prompted to rasterise the type layer. Once it's rasterised, the text can't be edited like regular text can, because it will now be considered an object instead of text. You can get around this by selecting **Layer > New Layer** *and adding all non-text lines and objects there.*

6. Click the down arrow next to the font window and select a font. I've been using Arial, but there are many others. Select a font you like.
7. Click the down arrow for font style (it might be greyed out depending on the font you've chosen), and make a selection if applicable. The choices differ depending on the font chosen, but can include Bold, Italic, Regular, Bold Italic, Roman, and others.
8. Click on the colour window and select a colour from the Color Picker. Click **OK** to return to the work area.
9. Click the tick in the Options bar to apply the text and attributes.

There are other options available, including setting the alignment of the text, warping the text, and choosing an anti-aliasing method. We'll talk about these soon.

Comparing Point Type and Paragraph Type

Point Type and Paragraph Type are two different ways to specify how characters will act inside the text's bounding box. When using **Point Type**, each line of text that you add is independent of the other lines; it never wraps to the next line. This means that if you run out of space in the work area, the letters that don't fit on the page won't show. Each text line entered using the Type tool creates a new layer (except when using the **Return** or **Enter** key on the same text layer).

When using **Paragraph Type**, all of the letters typed in wrap to new lines based on the size of the bounding box. Using this option, paragraphs of text can be entered and if more space is required, the bounding box can simply be resized. Figure 8.2 shows an example of this.

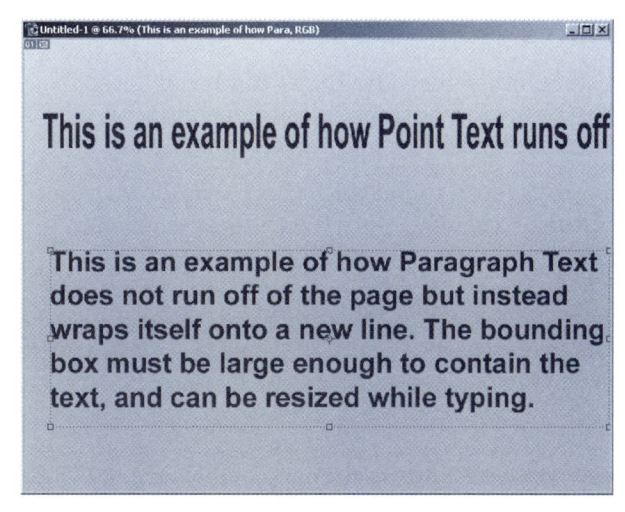

Figure 8.2 Point Type versus Paragraph Type.

You can switch from one type to the other easily:

1. Select the Type layer to convert in the Layers palette by clicking on it once.
2. Choose **Layer > Type > Convert to Point Text** or **Layer > Type > Convert to Paragraph Text**.
3. If you get a warning about some of the text being deleted, click **Cancel**. The warning says that all of the characters that overflow the bounding box will be deleted. Make sure you can see all of the text on the screen. You will have to select the **Move** tool and resize the bounding box until you can see all of the text. Once this is achieved, repeat step 2 to perform the conversion.

Adjusting type properties

Besides colour, size, font and style, other text attributes can be adjusted from the Options bar. There are anti-aliasing options, alignment options, and a toggle icon for switching between the Character and Paragraph palettes.

Anti-aliasing options allow you to smooth the edges of text and allow them to blend in better with the rest of the image. There are five options available:

- **None** – no anti-aliasing is applied;
- **Smooth** – the type appears somewhat smoother, but light;
- **Crisp** – the type appears somewhat sharp;
- **Strong** – the type appears heavy;
- **Sharp** – the type appears very sharp.

Figure 8.3 shows the difference between None and Sharp, which are at either end of the spectrum of choices. The edges of the sharp R are much smoother than the edges of the one with no anti-aliasing applied.

Using anti-aliasing improves the look of the font in most situations. There's always a trade-off though. The downside of using anti-aliasing is that it increases the number of colours in the image, since it adds pixels for blending the font with the background. In solid colour images like the one in Figure 8.3, this is not as big a problem as blending text with a photo of multiple colours. More colours mean larger files, and for online work, larger files result in longer download times.

There are several aligning options too, including **Left Align Text**, **Center Text**, and **Right Align Text**. To align text left, right or centred, click one of these options.

8: Adding type

Figure 8.3 Anti-aliasing at work.

The Character and Paragraph palettes

The other two options for adjusting type properties are the Character and Paragraph palettes. These can be opened from the Options bar (see Figure 8.1 and the Toggle) or from **Window > Character** and **Window > Paragraph**. Figure 8.4 shows the Character and Paragraph palettes, which have been opened from the Options bar. Using these palettes, you can precisely adjust how your typed characters will look on the page.

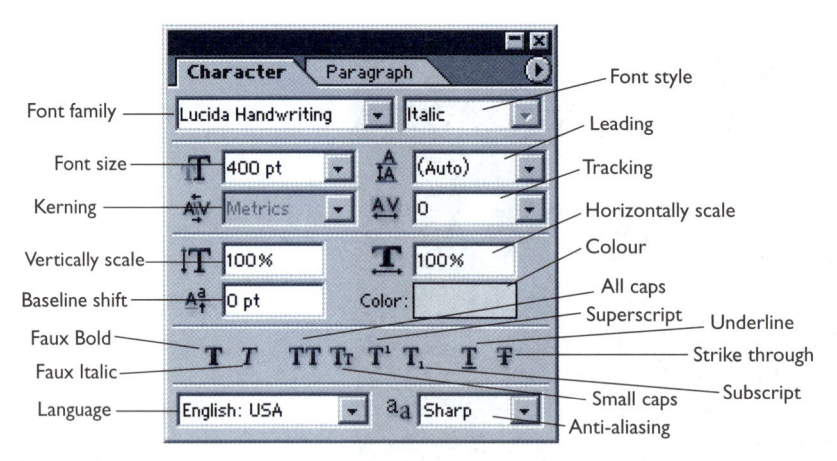

Figure 8.4 The Character and Paragraph palettes.

The Character palette

In the **Character** palette shown in Figure 8.4, notice that Lucida Handwriting is chosen, the font size is 400 pt, the anti-aliasing is Sharp, and the colour is a light mauve. These are the settings I configured in the Options bar for the image in Figure 8.3. You can configure options in this palette to change the common attributes of text in your text layers, such as colour, font, size and alignment, and also to change attributes such as kerning, leading, tracking and baseline shift, and so on.

Kerning determines how much space there is between specific letter pairs. Letter pairs like AV and Ky often seem out of sync with the other letters in text because of how the sides of the letter pairs align with each other. Kerning can be used to increase or decrease the space to remove this natural occurrence. **Tracking** keeps equal amounts of space across an entire range of letters, such as a paragraph. **Leading** is the amount of space in between lines of text. **Baseline Shift** is used to specify how far above or below the text appears from its normal baseline.

To apply any of these options, select the Type tool and open the Character palette. Using Figure 8.4 as a guide:

1. To apply kerning, click with the Type tool in between the two letters you wish to set the kerning for. In the Character palette, locate the kerning options (the icon has a capital A and V on it), and type a positive number to move characters apart or a negative number to move them together. You can also select a number from the drop-down list. Choose **Metric** to use the automatic kerning of the selected font.
2. To apply leading, select the lines of text to change by highlighting it using the Type tool. Type in a new number or choose one from the list. Larger numbers increase the distance between lines, smaller numbers decrease it.
3. To apply tracking, select the lines of text to change by highlighting it using the Type tool. Choose a new number from the list or type in a number of your own. Smaller numbers decrease space between letters, larger numbers increase space between letters.
4. To apply baseline shift, select the letters to shift above or below the normal baseline of the text. Type in a positive number to raise the letters, or type in a negative number to lower them. In Figure 8.5, the second Baseline Shift text has letters shifted above the normal baseline.

Figure 8.5 shows some examples.

Look back at Figure 8.4. There are other options in the Character palette, such as scaling, and applying styles such as Faux Bold, All Caps, Small Caps, etc. You can experiment with these by selecting the text with the mouse and the Type tool, and applying the styles.

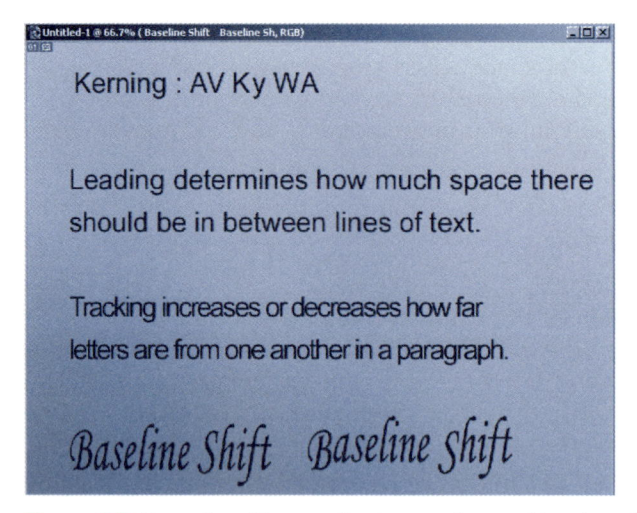

Figure 8.5 Examples of kerning, leading, tracking and baseline shift.

The Paragraph palette
The **Paragraph** palette is used to set options that apply to entire paragraphs of text, such as alignment, the indentation, and how much space there should be between lines of type.

To apply changes to paragraphs using this palette:

1. Select the paragraph for formatting by either clicking inside of it, or by choosing the **Type** layer in the Layers palette. You can also select paragraphs using the mouse and the Type tool.

2. Click on the **Paragraph** tab in the Character/Paragraph palette that is still on the screen, or choose **Window > Paragraph** to open it. Hover the mouse over each of the icons in the Paragraph palette to see what each icon does.
3. Choose from the justification choices for aligning text left, centre and right, type in a number to indent the paragraph or the lines in it, and set paragraph spacing by entering a value for **Space Before** and **Space After**. Each can be configured from the icons in this palette.
4. Place or remove the tick from the **Hyphenation** checkbox to specify whether words should be hyphenated when text wraps to a new line.

Click on the right arrow in the Character and Paragraph palettes to see additional options.

Other type options

Type can be selected using the Move tool and moved around the image like any other object. It can be resized, rotated and stretched. To edit text like an object, choose the **Type** layer from the Layers palette, and then choose the **Move** tool. A bounding box will appear around the text, which allows you to move and otherwise edit the text by size. Move the mouse outside the box to rotate the text.

Right-click on the text to see additional options such as **Scale**, **Skew**, **Flip Horizontal** and **Flip Vertical**. There are also rotate options. When the Move tool is chosen, the Options bar changes too. From the Options bar, you can change the height and width of the object, its centre rotation point, and so on.

Warping type

Warping type is fast and easy. It's a great way to make the text stand out, or form a shape. In the following example, we'll use some of the skills learned so far to create a business card with warped type. If you only want to warp type, then skip to step 6.

1. Choose **File > New** and create a new file that is 640 × 480, white background and RGB colour. Name the file *'Business Card'*.
2. Choose a background for your card. It can be a gradient from **Layer > New Fill Layer > Gradient**, a fill layer from **Layer > New Fill Layer > Solid Color**, or a pattern from **Layer > New Fill Layer > Pattern**. See Chapter 7 for more information on gradients. You can also choose a picture to serve as the background by starting with an existing file rather than a new one. You'll be adding text over the top of it, so make sure whatever you choose isn't too busy or dark.
3. Add any other images to the file by opening up additional images and copying and pasting to this image (Chapter 3), or choose a custom shape from the **Custom Shape** tool in the Toolbox (Chapter 4).
4. Add the text to your card using the techniques learned in this chapter.
5. Select the line of text to warp by selecting it from the Layers palette or choosing it with the mouse and the Type tool.
6. Click the **Warp Type** icon in the Options bar. Figure 8.6 shows the file I'm working on and the **Warp Text** dialogue box. The **Style** choices are showing.
7. Select the type of warp to apply from this dialogue box, then configure the settings. You can preview the changes as you make them. Figure 8.7 shows my final creation. Use the Move tool to reposition the text if necessary.

In Figure 8.7, I used a radial gradient layer, added two custom shapes using the Custom Shape tool, and added text. After the text was warped, I moved the text into position with the Move tool.

8: Adding type 163

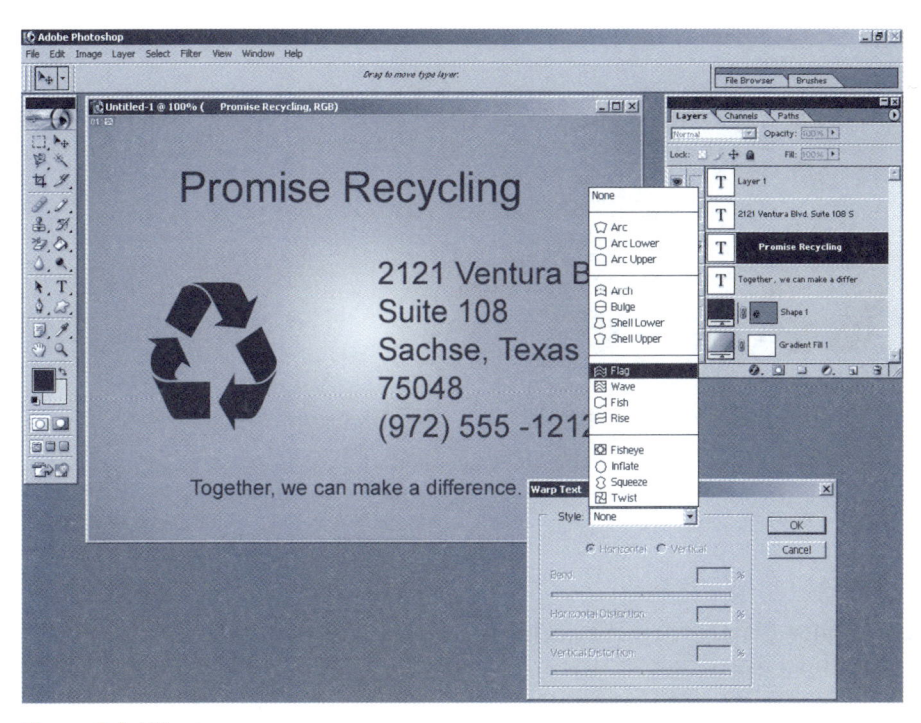

Figure 8.6 Warping text.

Figure 8.7 Creating a business card and warping text.

Rasterising type

As mentioned briefly earlier, text layers can only contain text. If you want to add something other than text to a text layer such as a stroke using a painting tool, adding a filter, or other similar item, you'll be prompted to rasterise the layer first. Rasterising the layer makes its text uneditable, so you'll want to do this only after you're sure the text is the way you want it.

Most of the time, I only rasterise text when I want to do something to a completed text layer and have been prompted that I must rasterise first. However, it is quite simple to rasterise the text layer manually. Just select the layer from the Layers palette, and choose **Layer > Rasterize > Type**. The layer can also be rasterised by right-clicking on the layer in the Layers palette and choosing **Rasterise Layer**.

Once rasterised, the text layer is like any other layer, and can be edited in the same way. The layer can be copied, duplicated, resized, filtered, painted on, stretched, and so on.

Summary

In this chapter you learned to add text (also called type) to an image using the Type tool. You learned about Point Text and Paragraph Text, and changing from one to the other. You also learned what attributes of text can be changed, including colour, size, font, kerning, tracking, leading, and so on. You learned to warp and rasterise text as well.

Using filters 9

What are filters?
Targeting selections and layers
Applying filters
Getting painterly
Adding distortion
Playing with light
Trying textures
Tips and tricks
Summary

Photoshop 7.0 offers a variety of filters that can be used to apply special effects to artwork, such as changing the look of an image from a photograph to a watercolour, coloured pencil, charcoal or sketch, to changing the look of image by distorting it, adding dust and scratches, or even adding a texture such as mosaic tiles or stained glass. There are so many filters to choose from, you might never apply even half of them!

What are filters?

You can buy a physical filter for your camera to create special effects while taking a photograph. These can include applying a halo or fog around the subject, polarising, softening, enhancing a colour or light, or even distorting. If you don't want to purchase these filters for your camera, however, you can apply them later using Photoshop 7.0's built-in filters. Besides these basic filters, special filters can also be applied.

Photoshop's filters are many, and include such filters as Watercolor, Film Grain, Sponge, Blur, Ink Outlines, Zig Zag, Clouds, Lens Flare, and Chalk and Charcoal. Most of these effects you can't get with physical camera filters, and thus enable you to transform images into anything but a 'regular' photo.

Targeting selections and layers

Filters can be applied to selections or to entire layers. Because applying filters is resource-intensive (i.e. uses a lot of RAM), it is best to choose a small selection instead of an entire layer when experimenting. To select a part of an image, use one of the selection tools (Chapter 3) or select the entire layer by choosing it from the Layers palette and choosing **Select > All** from the menu bar. Once the selection has been made, you are ready to apply a filter.

Applying filters

This is where it starts to get funky! Choose a photograph you'd like to apply a filter to, and open it up in Photoshop 7.0. Follow the directions in the next few sections to apply different filters to it. We'll start with some painting filters, move to distortion filters, experiment with some lighting filters, and try some textures.

Getting painterly

There are several options for filters that will make the image you are transforming look painted. Some are called Artistic filters, some are Brush Strokes filters, and some are Sketch filters. You can experiment with all of those here.

To apply a painting filter:

1. Use a selection tool to select part of the image, or choose the layer from the Layers palette and use **Select > All** to select the entire layer.
2. Choose **Filter > Artistic > Watercolor**.
3. From the **Watercolor** dialogue box that appears (shown in Figure 9.1), move the sliders to obtain the desired effect. Move the **Brush Detail** slider up to increase the painting detail, or move the brush down for more watercolour effect.
4. Click the – and + buttons to zoom in and out.
5. Move the **Shadow Intensity** slider to increase or decrease the shadows in the image.
6. Move the **Texture** slider to increase or decrease the watercolour's texture. Moving up increases the effect, moving down decreases it.

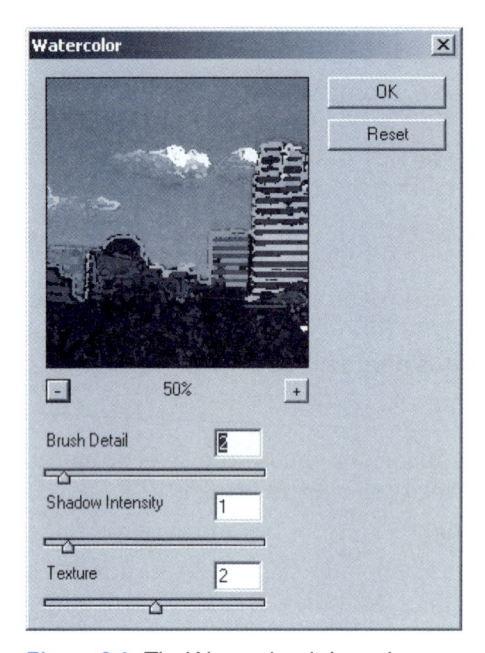

Figure 9.1 The Watercolor dialogue box.

7. Click **OK** when finished. Figure 9.2 shows a before-and-after shot.
8. To experiment with other Artistic filters, choose **Edit > Step Backward** or **Edit > Undo Watercolor** and apply some different filters.

Figure 9.3 shows the same image with the Artistic filter **Palette Knife** applied.

9: Using filters | 171

Figure 9.2 Applying a watercolour effect to a photograph.

Figure 9.3 Palette Knife Artistic filter applied to the same photograph.

Brush Strokes filters are applied in the same manner as Artistic filters. They are accessed from **Filter > Brush Stroke > <filter name>**. Some of my favourites include:

- **Accented Edges** – emphasises the edges in an image and depending on the settings can make them look like they are outlined with chalk or with a black paintbrush.
- **Angled Strokes** – redraws the image using diagonal paint strokes. Parts of the image are drawn one way, other parts in another way, giving a freshly painted look to the image.

- **Ink Outlines** – redraws the photo using pen and ink.
- **Spatter** – gives an airbrushed look to the image, as if the image had been spray painted with a can of paint.

To apply a Sketch filter, choose **Filter > Sketch ><name of filter>**. There are lots of sketch options including **Chalk and Charcoal**, **Graphic Pen**, **Photocopy**, **Stamp** and **Water Paper**. Figure 9.4 shows **Filter > Sketch > Water Paper** performed on a photograph of some plants outside a restaurant. This type of filtered image could be used as a background for a menu, sign or advertisement, and the opacity could be changed on this image to increase the water paper look.

You can always undo a filter from the Edit menu.

Adding distortion

Distort filters allow you to distort an image in various ways. There are lots of distort filters including filters to make the image look 'softer' (**Diffuse Glow**), to make the image appear as it would behind different types of glass (**Glass**), to make the image appear as if it's underwater (**Ocean Ripple**), and to give the object a 3D look (**Spherize**). There are others too, and the best way to see what each do is to experiment with them.

1. Use a selection tool to select part of the image, or choose the layer from the Layers palette and use **Select > All** to select the entire layer.
2. Choose **Filters > Distort > Diffuse Glow**. Use the **+** and **−** to zoom in and out, and set the sliders for **Graininess**, **Glow Amount** and **Clear Amount** to obtain the right effect. Click **OK** when finished.

Figure 9.4 Using the Water Paper filter.

Choose **Edit > Undo**, and try some other filters. Most are applied in the same way; they just have different options. There are so many different distort filters that it would be difficult to go through them all, but some of them do stand out.

Try **Spherize** to give the image a 3D look, as shown in Figure 9.5. Choose **Twirl** to turn or twist the image selection, as shown in Figure 9.6. Try **Pinch** to pinch the middle of the object inward, and give a concave look. Try **Zig Zag** to add ridges throughout the image, as shown in Figure 9.7.

9: Using filters

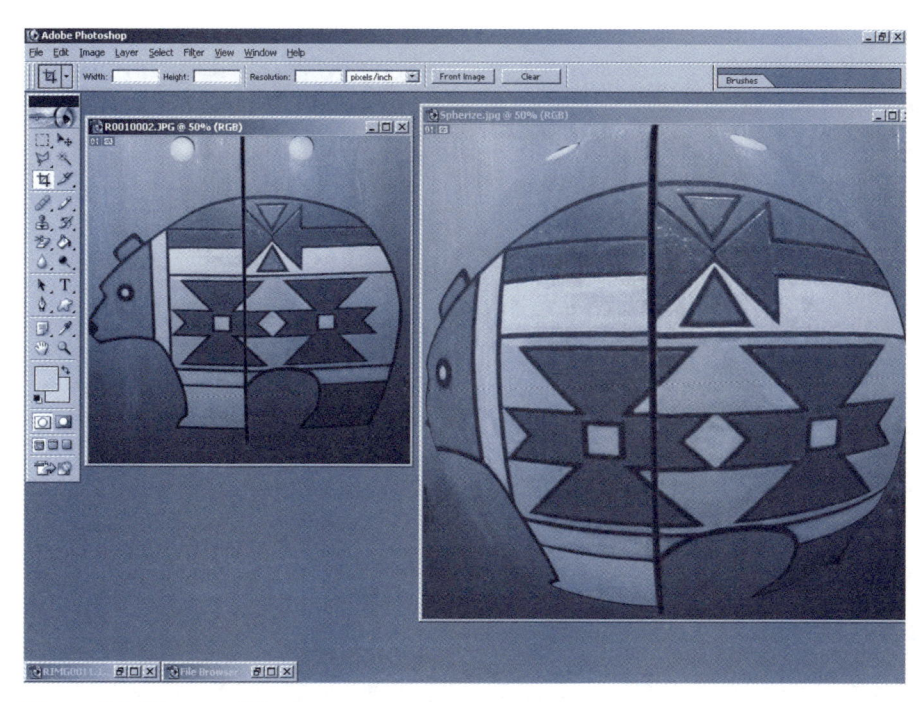

Figure 9.5 Distort > Spherize.

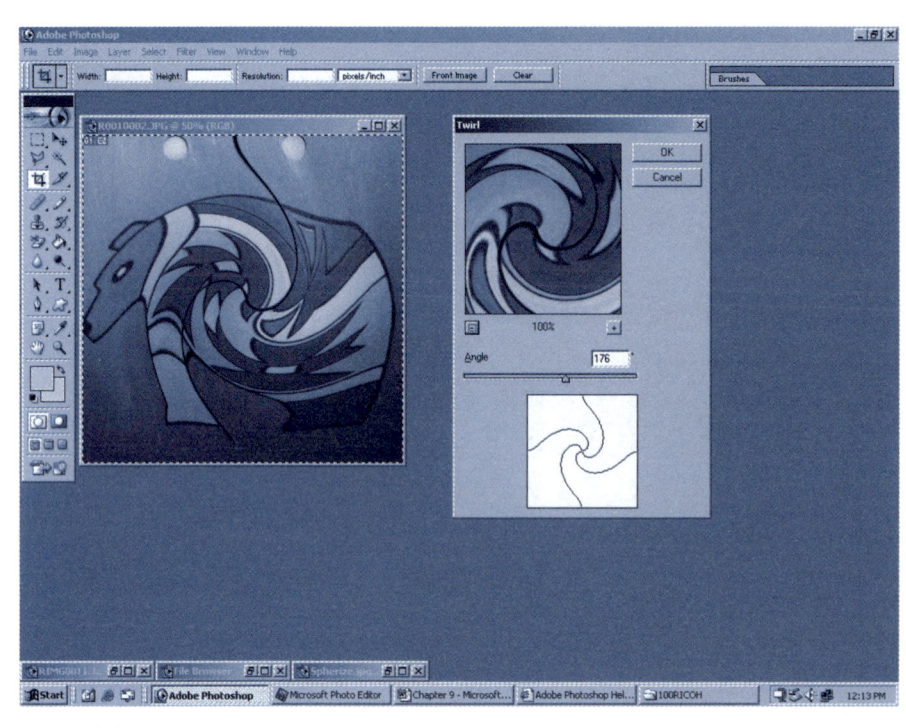

Figure 9.6 Distort > Twirl.

Figure 9.7 Distort > Zig Zag.

Playing with light

There are lots of filters for changing the amount of light in an image or layer. Figure 9.8 shows the dialogue box for one of them: **Filter > Render > Lighting Effects**.

Using this dialogue box you can apply multiple types of lighting options, including moving the direction from where the light is shining, choosing from **Spotlight**, **Omni** or **Directional**, changing **Intensity** and **Focus**, and so on. In Figure 9.9, Spotlight has been applied and intensity has been increased, to give the photo a different look. This same filter can be used on family photos to give a professional quality look by applying lighting from various directions.

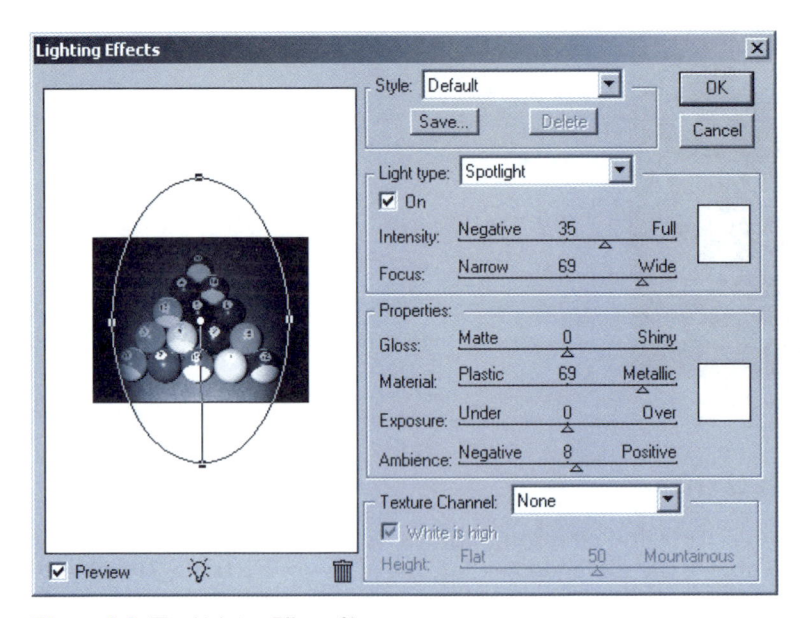

Figure 9.8 The Lighting Effects filter.

There are other lighting effects worth trying:

- **Filter > Render > Lens Flare** – allows you to recreate a lens flare by specifying where the lens flare is to occur in the image. This is achieved by moving the cross-hairs in the **Lens Flare** dialogue box.
- **Filter > Render > Clouds** (or) **Difference Clouds** – both produce cloud patterns that make the image seem foggy or cloudy. From the **Edit** menu, choose **Fade Clouds** to edit the opacity of the new filter's effect.

9: Using filters

Figure 9.9 Applying lighting effects.

- **Filter > Stylize > Glowing Edges** – adds a neon glow to the edges of the image. Figure 9.10 shows this filter in action.
- **Filter > Stylize > Find Edges** – finds the edges of an image and lightens the areas around them. See Figure 9.11.

Of course, there are lots more filters, some of which do change the lighting of the image you are working with. Experiment as long as time allows so that you have a good feel for what's available.

While distorting might be fun for you, keep in mind that your mother probably won't be as thrilled with the pinched or twirled faces of your kids as you are. For her, consider an effect that makes them look angelic instead.

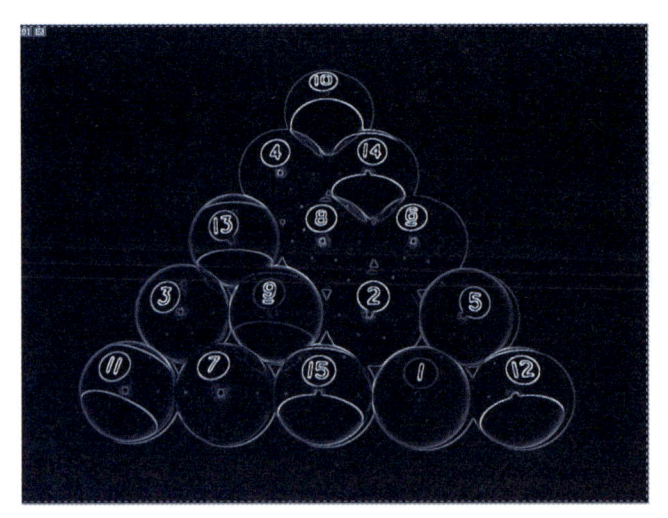

Figure 9.10 Using the Glowing Edges filter.

Trying textures

Textures can be used to add neat effects to your images too. There are several of them, as with the other filters. They include:

- **Filter > Texture > Craquelure** – changes the surface to a plaster-type texture, which adds cracks and lines of texture to the image.
- **Filter > Texture > Grain** – allows you to make the image grainy using all kinds of grain types including regular, soft, sprinkles, speckle, and so on. You can change the intensity and contrast as well.

9: Using filters 181

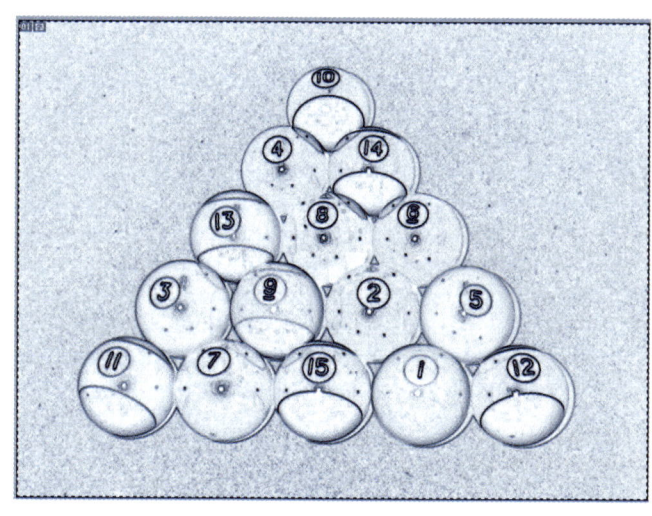

Figure 9.11 Finding edges.

- **Filter > Texture > Mosaic Tiles** – redraws the image so that it looks like it has been created using mosaic tiles. You can change the tile size, grout width and lightness.
- **Filter > Texture > Patchwork** – changes the image so that it looks like a patchwork quilt. Square size and relief can be configured.
- **Filter > Texture > Stained Glass** – changes the image so that it looks like it was created on stained glass. Cell size, border thickness and relief can be configured.

Relief adjusts the depth of the texture.

- **Filter > Texture > Texturizer** – allows you to choose from various textures including brick, burlap, canvas and sandstone. Scaling, relief and light direction can be configured.

To apply a texture and see its most basic attributes:

1. Open a new file with RGB colour and a white background.
2. Choose one of the filters available to see its effect on a plain white canvas. Edit the filter using the options in the dialogue box.
3. Choose **Edit > Undo** and apply the other filters one at a time.
4. Next, open an image with multiple colours and apply the filters again. Each of the filters takes into account the colours in the image and produces an effect based on the settings in the dialogue boxes. Change them as desired to get the wanted effect. Figure 9.12 shows the filter **Mosaic Tiles** applied to an image. Both the before and after shots are shown.

Tips and tricks

Before reading my list of tips and tricks, make sure that you've fully experimented with all of the filters at least once. It's important that you know exactly what filters are available, and have some idea as to what each can do for you.

With that out of the way, try these tips and tricks:

- Don't worry that you'll apply a filter and be stuck with it; you can always undo from the Edit menu.
- After you've applied a filter, use brushes and the Pen and Pencil tools to touch up small areas of it. Use the zoom tools to zoom in on particular sections of the image.

Figure 9.12 Using the Mosaic Tiles filter.

- If you are really serious about becoming a Photoshop 7.0 expert and artist, consider purchasing a graphics tablet for more precise drawing.
- Save your work between steps so you'll have something to revert to if needed. Consider saving under multiple names too.
- Experiment with each of the sliders in the dialogue boxes before applying. The default settings aren't necessarily the best, and only by experimenting with the settings will you get a better idea of the program's capabilities.

- Free up some memory before you begin applying filters by selecting **Edit > Purge > All**. This will clear the RAM so that operations with the filters will occur more quickly.
- Try applying filters to a blank canvas and using that canvas as a background for other artwork, such as signs, flyers or business cards.
- When applying filters, move the sliders all the way to the left to see the effect, then all the way to the right. For Artistic filters, this technique is extremely helpful in getting the filter setting just right.
- If a choice in the Filter menu has ellipses after it (...), then a dialogue box will appear; if not, the filter will be applied without options.
- After applying a filter, choose **Edit > Fade** to change the opacity of the filter.
- Click on the layer with the filter in the Layers palette to change fill and opacity if the layer is to serve as one of multiple layers.
- Combine multiple filters for greater effects. For instance, use the **Texture > Texturizer > Canvas** filter to apply a texture, then use another filter to add effect.

Summary

In this chapter you learned all about filters, including how to apply filters and what filters are available. In particular, we focused on painting, distortion, light and texture filters, although there are lots more available. Multiple filters can be applied to either layers or layer selections.

Printing, saving, and Web-readying

10

Printing your work
Setting up the page
The Print dialogue box
Setting print options
Printing
Saving your work
Setting preferences for saving files
A few words about file formats
Exploring common file formats
Saving in Photoshop file formats
Optimising for the web
Using the save for Web command
Summary

While you might not think you need some of the printing options detailed in this chapter, read through them all anyway so you know they're available if you ever do need them.

Once you've created a file, image or piece of artwork, edited it, and have everything just right, you'll probably want to print it out so that you can share it with others. At the very least, you'll want to save it. In this chapter, you'll learn how to do all of these things, as well as how to optimise your photos, images and artwork for the Web.

Printing your work

Printing is quite simple using Photoshop 7.0. In fact, it can be just as easy as printing from a word-processing application. What's different is that instead of printing black and white text, you're printing artwork and images. Photoshop 7 does more than print images though; it can also be used to print four-colour separations and negatives and to put images on films and speciality papers for professional printing. Many of the options most users will never employ, unless you are in the business of printing magazines, posters, signs or business cards, if you do screen printing (putting images on T-shirts, hats, etc.), or are into sublimation (putting images on coffee mugs, golf balls, etc.). Keeping this in mind, let's learn how to 'just' print, how to optimise our images for different kinds of printing, and about the other options that can be configured for professional print-outs.

Setting up the page

The first step when printing is to set up the page. To see the options for Page Setup as shown in the dialogue box in Figure 10.1, click on **File > Print With Preview**, then click the **Page Setup** button. You can also open this dialogue box by choosing **File > Page Setup**.

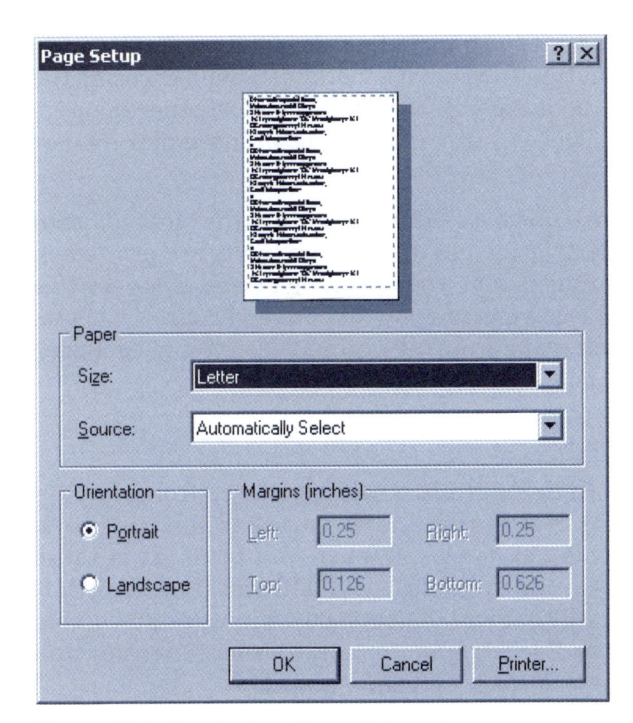

Figure 10.1 Use the Page Setup dialogue box to set page options before printing.

*When printing, use the **File > Print With Preview** dialogue box. By doing so, you can not only access the Page Setup and Printer dialogue boxes and options, but also work with the additional options detailed in the next section.*

There are several options that can be set, including choosing and configuring the printer using the **Printer** button (if you have more than one), choosing the paper size and from what tray the paper will be selected, and whether the page will be portrait or landscape. There is also an area to configure margins for custom printing.

Portrait prints are printed up and down on the page, and are the most common for documents, faxes and artwork or images. Landscape prints are printed on the paper longways, and are most common when printing images of scenery. To set any of these options, click the down arrows by the Size and Source windows and select the desired option. Click the **Printer** button to select and configure the printer. The Print dialogue box will be introduced next.

The Print dialogue box

The **Print** dialogue box is shown in Figure 10.2 and is accessed from the **File > Print With Preview** choice. Notice that there is a tick in the box **Show More Options**; make sure this box is ticked when you print. It is these remaining options that make printing in Photoshop 7 different from the printing you are probably already used to. Print dialogue boxes in word-processing programs don't offer items like Background, Screen, Border, Transfer and Bleed, so let's get familiar with what these options achieve.

- **Background** – this button brings up the Color Picker, and is used to choose a background that will be printed on the page outside the image area. This can be used to place a 'frame' around the picture, which is sometimes helpful when printing slides for a slideshow, or for a picture for mum and dad of the grandchildren. This option doesn't change the image at all.

10: Printing, saving and Web-readying 189

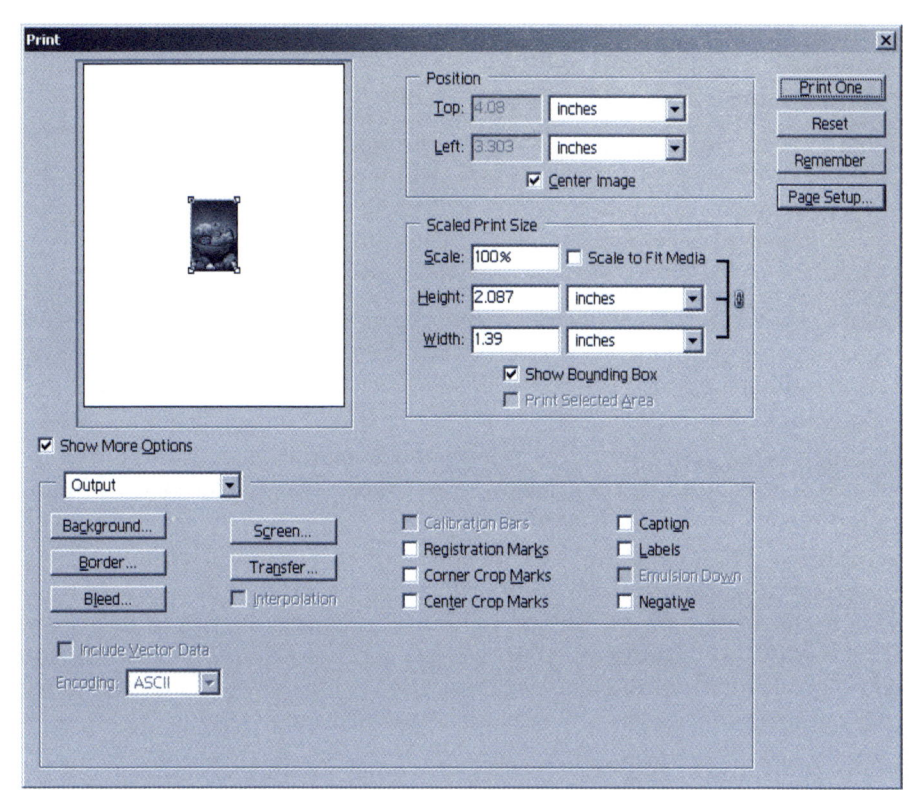

Figure 10.2 Use the Print dialogue box to set advanced print options.

- **Border** – lets you place a border around the image. Unlike the background, the border is black and the width of the border can be selected. The width can be set using inches, millimetres or points.

From here on, the print options become a bit more specialised. Generally, only professional printers, print shops, screen printers, those who do colour separations for printing on specialised films, and those who produce images for use with mechanical presses use the rest of the remaining print options. If you aren't into any of this, most of these won't apply to your printing needs.

- **Bleed** – lets you print crop marks inside the image. Usually, these marks are placed outside the image. Crop marks are used to trim the image. Like the Border option, the width can be set using inches, millimetres or points.
- **Screen** – when printing out film for screens for use with mechanical screen printing presses, this option lets you set the screen frequency and dot shape for each screen used in the process. Use this setting if you are producing camera-ready artwork for a print shop.
- **Transfer** – when printing out film for screens for use with mechanical screen printing presses, there are usually some dots lost or dots gained when the image is printed on the film or vellum. This causes the final output to be off by design, by line or by colour. If you are using an older PostScript printer for your film, consider tweaking the options here in addition to the other options available for screens and screen printers.

There are some other options too, and they can be set by placing a tick in the box to apply them. They include:

- **Calibration Bars** – if the paper is large enough to contain the image and has room left over, you can add calibration bars added to the page. These are best used when printing CMYK colour separations for use in creating screens or other printing templates. The calibration is shown in increments of 10% and can be used to check the colour output of the print device.
- **Caption** – prints a caption for a photo as entered into the File Info dialogue box. Caption text always prints as 9-point Helvetica plain type and can be added using the **File > File Info** dialogue box as shown in Figure 10.3.
- **Crop Marks** – adds crop marks where the page should be trimmed. This is different from the Bleed command, because these marks are on the inside the image, while the marks used with the Bleed command are outside. Crop marks can be added to the centre and/or the edges of the image.
- **Emulsion Down** – when printing on certain films or papers, such as those used with heat transfer machines, the image is placed on the film emulsion side down, making the image appear in reverse on the page. Tick this option when using these types of papers.
- **Interpolation** – if printing a low-resolution image, tick this box to reduce the rough and irregular appearance of the image's edges that occurs during printing. This feature won't work if your PostScript printer doesn't support the feature.
- **Labels** – prints the filename on the printed page, just above the image.
- **Negative** – used to print the negative (the inverted version) of the image. Use this option when printing film negatives.
- **Registration Marks** – a bit like crop marks, these marks can be added to the image and are used mainly for aligning the colour separations during the physical print process.

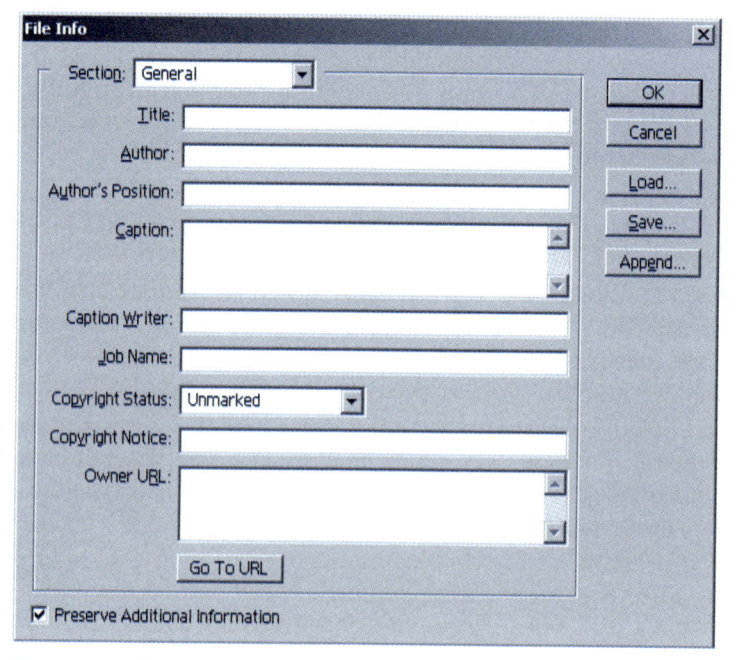

Figure 10.3 Using the **File > File Info** dialogue box for adding a caption to a printed image.

- **Encoding** – by default, the printer driver transmits binary information to PostScript printers; however, you can choose to transfer image data using JPEG or ASCII encoding.

While you might not have any use for most of these options, other people will. If you're just starting your own print business for instance, you'll find experimenting with these options and your PostScript printer quite rewarding.

Setting print options

Figure 10.4 shows the **Print Options** dialogue box. You can open this dialogue box by clicking on the **Print** button in the Print dialogue box shown in Figure 10.2, or by choosing **File>Print**.

Here, you can do things specific to your printer, including printing front-to-back, printing additional copies, and accessing your own printer's properties. Click the **Properties** button to set quality settings, set colour settings, define paper sources or types, and so on. Different printers offer different options; if you are confused about any of these options, consult your printer's documentation.

*If you just want to print one copy, choose **File > Print One Copy**. You won't have the option to configure anything, and the file will print with the default settings.*

Printing

Once you have all of the Page Setup and Print Options configured, you're finally ready to print!

To print a document:

1. From the **File** menu, choose **Print With Preview**. Place a tick in the **Show More Options** checkbox.
2. Make configuration changes in the Print dialogue box by placing a tick in the available boxes for **Calibration Bars**, **Crop Marks**, **Registration Marks**, etc., and set the background, border and other qualities as well.
3. Click the **Page Setup** button.

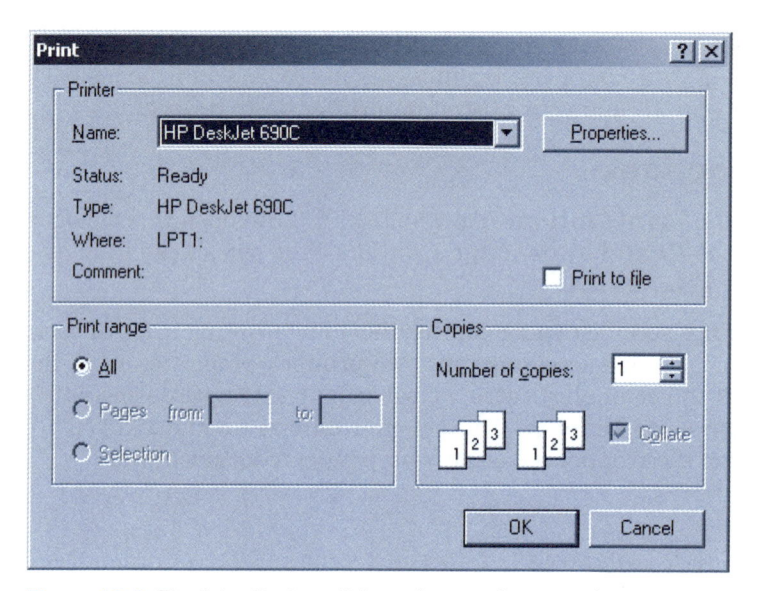

Figure 10.4 The Print Options dialogue box can be opened in two ways.

4. From the Page Setup dialogue box, make the appropriate choices for **Size** and **Source**, by clicking the down arrow by each window and making a selection. Choose the appropriate orientation using the radio buttons. Click **OK**.
5. Back at the Print dialogue box, click the **Print** button.
6. Select the printer you want to use from the list in the new Print dialogue box.
7. Select the number of copies and in what order they should print, the print range, and make any other configurations necessary from the new Print dialogue box. The options will vary from printer to printer.

8. Click the **Properties** button next to the printer name.
9. From the printer's Properties dialogue box, choose the quality and colour settings, and any other configurations as needed. (For help here, you'll have to refer to your own printer's documentation.)
10. Click **OK** in the printer Properties dialogue box, and click **OK** again in the Print dialogue box. The page will begin printing.

Saving your work

You probably already know how to save a file; in fact, you've probably already saved hundreds of files while using word-processing or database programs. Saving in Photoshop 7 is pretty much the same as saving in any other program, except that you have a few more choices. Figure 10.5 shows the **Save As** dialogue box. This is what you'll be using to learn the different ways of saving a file.

There are two ways to save a file: the **File > Save** and **File > Save As** commands. There's absolutely no difference between the two if you are saving a file for the first time, as both bring up the Save As dialogue box shown in Figure 10.5. However, if the file has been saved previously, **File > Save** simply saves on top of the previously saved file without offering the dialogue box at all.

The Save As dialogue box is used to save a file and state where it should be saved, what file format it should use, and to create a file name. You'll want to use **File > Save As** when you are changing anything concerning how the file was saved the first time. For instance, I like to save files in stages, especially after a major change, so that I can go back to a specific time and place if I need to. I name the files File_Name1, File_Name2, File_Name3, etc. This way, I have several copies of the same file in different stages of construction.

*Once you hit **OK** in the Print dialogue box in step 9, the page will begin to print. If you aren't ready, don't select the OK button; instead, press **Cancel**, and continue to set options, then choose the OK button when ready.*

*Notice in this screenshot that I've chosen the **My Pictures** folder as the place to save my files. In this folder, I've also created several other folders. Setting up the folders this way helps keep them organised, and makes pictures easy to find.*

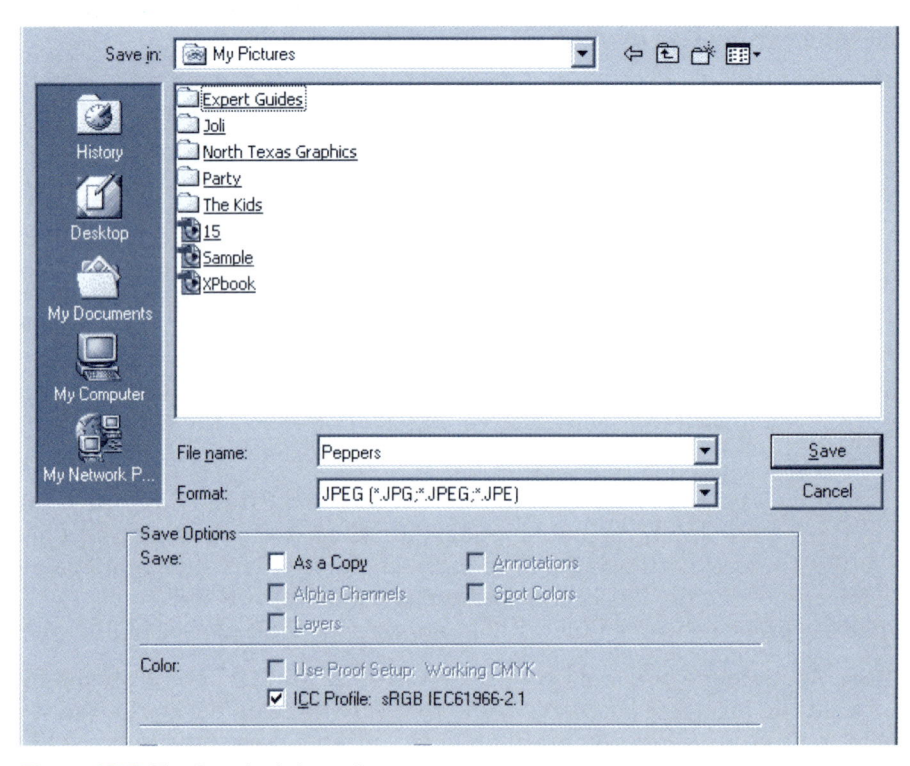

Figure 10.5 The Save As dialogue box.

To save a file for the first time:

1. Choose **File > Save As** or **File > Save**.
2. From the Save As dialogue box, type in a name for the file. File names should follow the naming conventions of your operating system.
3. Click the down arrow in the **Formats** window and choose the appropriate format. For more information on file formats, see later sections in this chapter.
4. To save the file as a copy, place a tick in the **Save As a Copy** checkbox.
5. To embed an ICC profile, place a tick in the **ICC Profile** checkbox. ICC profiles contain data concerning how the colour settings of a device stray from the standard. This ensures that colours are accurately transferred from one device (like a monitor or computer) to a second device (such as a printer). Because no two devices are likely to be calibrated perfectly, ticking this box is a good idea when it is available. It is not available for all file types.
6. Click **Save**.

To save quickly a file that's been saved previously, select the **File > Save** command. No dialogue box will appear, and the new data will be written over the existing file and will replace it.

In this section, we talked about how to print and save files created in and using Photoshop 7.0. Photoshop 7.0 comes with another program, called ImageReady. Printing and saving in ImageReady is a little different than with PhotoShop 7.0. ImageReady is a highly sophisticated program that is used to create Web graphics and animations. For now, we'll just focus on printing and saving in Photoshop 7.0.

Save your work regularly, perhaps every 10–15 minutes. That way you won't lose too much work if there's a power cut or a glitch in the program or if your computer crashes.

Setting preferences for saving files

When working with the Save As dialogue box, you probably noticed that there were specific defaults; for instance, the default file type is PSD, and the default folder for saving is Samples. When you make changes to these options, Photoshop 7.0 remembers, and offers you the last-used settings the next time you save. You can make changes to other default options through **Edit > Preferences > File Handling**. Figure 10.6 shows this dialogue box.

From here, you can change how image previews will be saved, how file extensions will be displayed, and whether or not you want to maximise backward compatibility and view advanced TIFF save options. You can also enable workgroup functionality, and allow users to view the file from the network server. The options here allow you to set never, always or to ask first. Go ahead and open this dialogue box, check the advanced TIFF options, and change the other preferences as desired. Click **OK**.

A few words about file formats

How do you know what file format to save in? There are so many, it's enough to confuse anyone! And, why do we need so many different formats anyway?

Let's begin with the last question. File formats are chosen to determine how the file will be saved. Formats determine how the file will be compressed, what programs will be able to open it, and how they will retain colour and resolution (among other things). Some formats save colours and resolution quite well but create large files, while others don't do such a good job with colour or resolution but create much smaller files. If you are trying to open a Web page, you'd probably rather get the page and its pictures up quickly and sacrifice a little

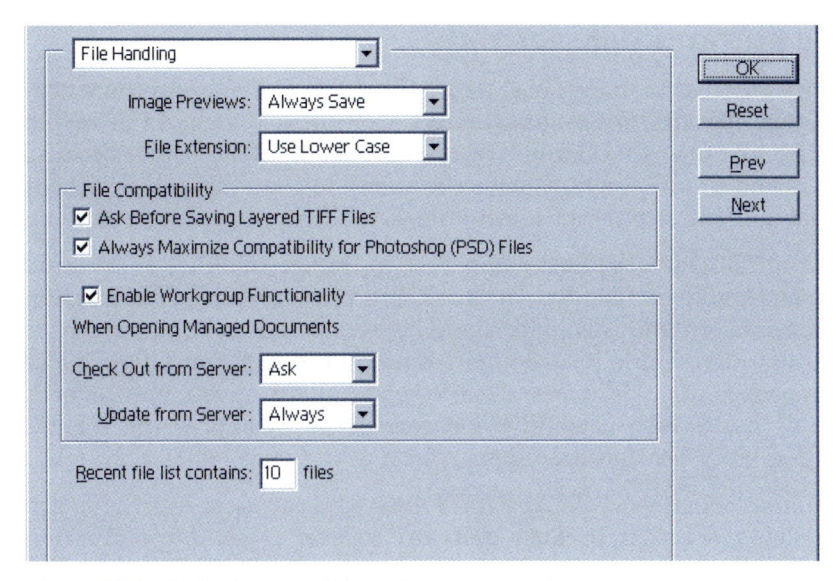

Figure 10.6 The Preferences dialogue box for saving files.

resolution, than to have to wait 20 minutes for the page to come up. Also, while your Aunt Mary will most likely be able to open a JPEG file, she won't be able to open a file saved in Photoshop's format unless she has the program on her system. Therefore, deciding on a file format can be quite an important task.

In the next couple of sections, we'll talk about the different file formats. You'll learn about TIFF, BMP, JPEG, PICT, GIF, EPS, DCS, PSD and PDF.

Exploring common file formats

Of the 30 or so choices you have for saving a file, there are a few that are considered 'common' formats. For sending images attached to e-mails or for saving to websites, for instance, JPEG and GIF are used most often. This is because most browsers and e-mail programs have the ability to open these files without any additional plug-ins or programs, meaning virtually anyone can open them.

The GIF and JPEG formats also compress the image, making them good choices for sending large files like artwork and photographs. Compression makes the file smaller, and this helps the images get from point A to point B much faster than they would if saved in a non-compressed form. This reduces how long a message with an image takes to send and download, and reduces the amount of bandwidth used in a network. When compressing images though, image quality is reduced, so there *is* a tradeoff for speed.

Another common format is TIFF. With TIFF files, you can compress the image and retain image resolution, because there are several 'lossless' compression options to choose from when saving. You can even save the TIFF file with a Zip option for reducing file size even more. This is a great option when the file is quite large.

BMP and PICT file formats are native to Windows and Macintosh systems respectively. Neither are that good at saving resolutions, and are generally used only for desktop wallpaper.

GIF is best suited for line art, drawings and images with only a few colours; JPEG is best for photographs.

When combining TIFF and Zip, make sure the recipient has Photoshop installed on their system. Otherwise, they might have trouble opening it. If they don't have Photoshop installed, you can still use TIFF, just don't Zip it too.

Saving in Photoshop file formats

There are several Photoshop file formats. These formats are the best to use when you are saving files created in Photoshop, because the format works well with layers and other Photoshop-specific tools.

These file types are really TIFF files with additional enhancements. Not only do these file types compress the image (make it smaller), but they also offer lossless compression.

The disadvantage of the Photoshop formats such as PSD is that the recipient must have Photoshop installed on their system to open the file. If you know that your recipient doesn't, then send in plain old TIFF, or choose JPEG or GIF.

There are four file types that are Photoshop-related: EPS, DCS, PSD and PDF. EPS stands for Encapsulated PostScript and the files must be printed on a PostScript printer. This file type can contain both vector and bitmap graphics, and is used to transfer PostScript artwork between graphics applications and to printers.

DCS is Desktop Color Separation and is also used with PostScript printers. This file type is used when you need to print out colour separations of CMYK images.

PSD is the default format and is most likely what you'll be choosing for editing and working with files. This format supports any work you'll do in Photoshop, including work using bitmap, greyscale, duotone, indexed colour, RGB, CMYK, etc.

Finally, PDF (Portable Document Format) files are used mainly for documents and text. This file type remembers and displays page layouts, fonts and graphics. PDF is a common format on the Internet, and is often used to quickly download large documents to a user's computer.

Lossless means that quality and colour attributes won't be lost, as compared with 'lossy' compression offered by JPEG and other file types.

Save photos and images in a Photoshop PSD format for your own use, and save again in JPEG or GIF when e-mailing the file to someone else.

In the table below, the differences between the file types and their characteristics are summarised. (Of course, there are lots more file types, but these are the ones you will likely use most often.)

File name	Characteristics	When to use
TIFF	Widely supported, offers lossless compression by retaining image clarity, colour and resolution.	For sending scanned images to professional print shops, when you need to compress.
Bitmap (BMP)	Native Windows format. Only supports up to 24-bit colour.	For desktop wallpaper.
PICT	Native Macintosh format. Supports 16-bit and 32-bit colour.	For desktop wallpaper.
JPEG	Widely supported, compresses, but loses image resolution, clarity and colour. Greatly reduces file size.	For e-mailing photographs or saving final versions of files. Also a good format for websites.
GIF	Widely supported, offers lossless compression, moderately reduces file size, 256 colours only.	For line drawings, logos and other images with few colours. A common e-mail format. Also a good format for websites.

PSD	Default Photoshop format for newly created images.	For saving and working with Photoshop images, photos and artwork.
PDF	Photoshop format for text and graphics.	Mainly for text documents.
EPS	Photoshop format for vector and bitmap images to transfer PostScript files between applications.	When sharing PostScript graphics files between applications.
DCS	Photoshop format for saving colour separations.	When printing out CMYK colour separations for spot colour or process colour on PostScript printers.

With this information in hand, you can now decide on the file type to save your file as. To summarise, use PSD to save your work while editing and creating your files. Once they are complete, either save them as PSD or in some other format. Choose JPEG to e-mail a photo, GIF to e-mail line art or logos, and TIFF to send to a professional printer or print shop. For saving four-colour separations, use DCS.

Optimising for the Web

Deciding on a file type for saving an image to your computer is pretty easy, especially in these days of 20 and 30 GB hard drives and 256 MB of RAM. With drives this big, choosing to compress an image to save a few megabytes of space isn't usually an issue. E-mailing an image is pretty easy too: just choose JPEG or GIF, and zip the file if desired. Saving an image for use on the Web though requires a little more thought.

Why optimise?
When a potential client, a family member, or any person visits your website, the pictures on that site have to be appealing, but at the same time display quickly. When saving images for the Web then, you must try to strike a balance between the size of the file (which affects how long it will take to download and display) and the quality of the image. You'll want to create the smallest size possible while retaining enough colour and resolution to display properly. JPEG and GIF are common file formats for this task, since both allow for compression and are widely accepted formats. PNG is also common, although we haven't talked about that much, but it is not as widely accepted as the first two, so we'll stick with those for now.

While the additional program that comes with Photoshop 7.0, ImageReady, can be used to optimise files for the Web, you can use and apply all of this program's file optimisation capabilities through the Photoshop Save For Web dialogue box.

Using the Save For Web command

Figure 10.7 shows the **Save For Web** dialogue box. Depending on the file format chosen, if it is a GIF, JPEG, or other format, the dialogue box will differ. The dialogue box has several palettes, arrows and options. To open this box, choose File > Save For Web.

10: Printing, saving and Web-readying

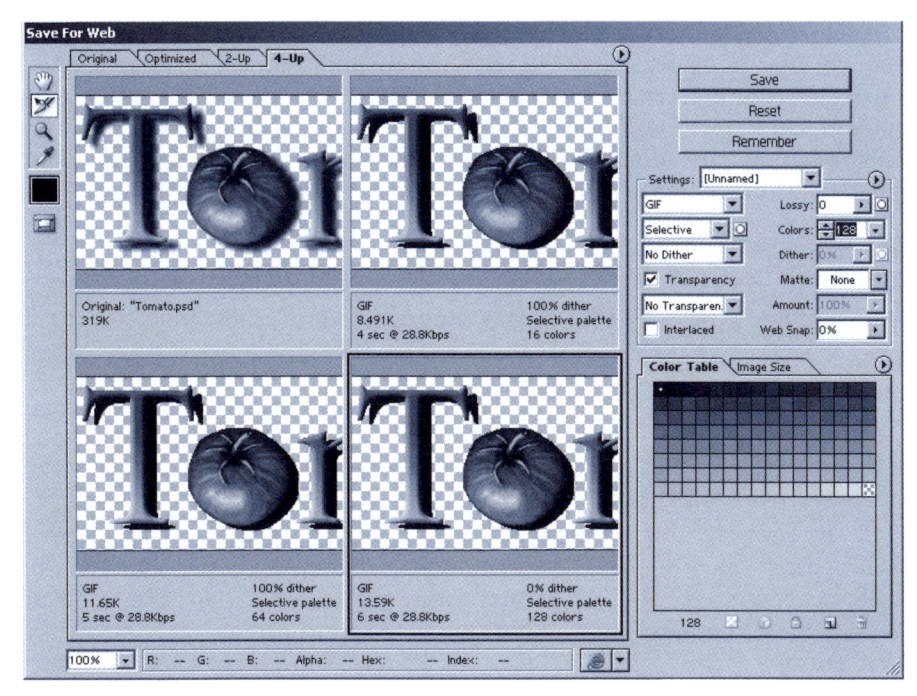

Figure 10.7 The Save For Web dialogue box can be used to optimise photos and images for the Web.

Remember, use GIF files when you have only a few colours in the image, or when you are saving line art, logos or illustrations with type; use JPEG or TIFF for photographs.

This dialogue box can be used for very precise optimisation tasks. For instance, you can preview images in different file formats and compare what looks best with how much time it will take to download the image using different connections. You can view multiple versions of the same file simultaneously. Transparency, matting, dithering, and so on can be set too, and you can create an HTML file for the image as well.

To learn how to optimise a JPEG file using the Save For Web dialogue box, work through the following steps:

1. Open the file Peppers.PSD from the Sample folder of Photoshop 7.0. It is a JPEG file.
2. Open the Save For Web dialogue box by selecting **File > Save For Web**.
3. Change how you view the files in the bottom left corner of the dialogue box by clicking on the down arrow there. Instead of 100% (or whatever is showing), select **Fit On Screen**.
4. Click on the **2-Up** and **4-Up** tabs to see multiple instances of the picture. Each picture can be selected and changed, and comparisons can then be made. Leave it on the 4-Up selection. After the 4-Up tab has been selected, choose a view you like from the bottom left corner options; 50% is good for this picture.
5. The first image is the original; we'll leave that one alone. Click on the second image. Notice that the name **JPEG** is showing in the **File Name** box, and **Medium** quality is chosen. In the **Quality** window, move the slider down from 30 to 10. You can also type in the number if desired. Compare how much time it takes to download the original photo (the first square) with this new setting in the second, and compare the quality of the picture. By

changing this setting from 30 to 10, you are telling the computer to compress the file by selectively discarding some of the data in the image. This of course results in colour and resolution degradation, but usually a setting between 10 and 30 is barely noticeable and reduces the size of the image considerably.

6. Click on the third image, and slide the **Quality** slider to 100. Notice how the quality improves, but the time it takes to download the file also changes considerably.

7. Click on the **Image Size** tab in the bottom right corner of the Save for Web dialogue box. Notice the size of the image. Change this to 200 × 300. Making the image size smaller greatly reduces the file size. Image size is the actual size of the photo, file size is how much space it takes up on your hard drive or website. Notice how the download time changes as the size of the file is reduced.

Here are some tips when optimising a JPEG image:

- Try to keep the download times short and the file size between 10K and 20K.
- Set the **Quality** option to configure the picture so that it is more detailed. High values cause the file size to grow, smaller values lessen the size.
- Tick the **Optimized** box if it is available to create an enhanced JPEG image while keeping the file size fairly small.
- Tick the **Progressive** box to allow the picture to come up in a viewer's browser in layers, to make the download time seem shorter and to show progress. This is similar to **Interlace**.
- Tick **Blur** and move the slider to blur the image. Usually a setting of less than 0.10 can't be detected, and lowers the file size by allowing it to be compressed more.

When saving a file that you've taken from the Samples folder, rename it first. If you don't, you'll save over the file that came with Photoshop 7.0. If this happens, you'll have to reinstall the samples from the CD-ROM.

Not all browsers support progressive JPEGs.

- Tick the **ICC Profile** box to preserve the colour profile of the image or the artwork. Doing so will increase the file size slightly.
- Use **Matte** to specify a colour for the part of the image that is transparent. Fully transparent pixels will be given the selected colour, which should be the colour of the Web page itself, and pixels that are partially transparent will be blended in.

Now, lets experiment with a GIF image, and look at some additional options.

1. Open the file Tomato.PSD from the Sample folder of Photoshop 7.0
2. Open the Save for Web dialogue box by selecting **File > Save For Web**.
3. For this GIF image, you can choose only colour schemes that use 256 or fewer colours. You can reduce colours to reduce the size of the image, thus making the download time faster. You can type in any number as well; you don't have to select one from the list. As you change the options in the **Colors** box, look at the quality and download times. Check out times and quality for 256 colors, 128 colors and 16 colors. See Figure 10.8.
4. Locate the **Dither** choices. Dithering is the process of simulating colours that need to be in the picture, but can't be because of limitations regarding the colour display of a computer. For instance, while your Web page might contain an image of more than 256 colours, the person viewing it might have a display card that supports only 256. Dithering simulates those colours when they aren't on the colour palette. Images that are mostly solid colours usually won't require dithering, but images with continuous colour like this photograph probably will.

10: Printing, saving and Web-readying 209

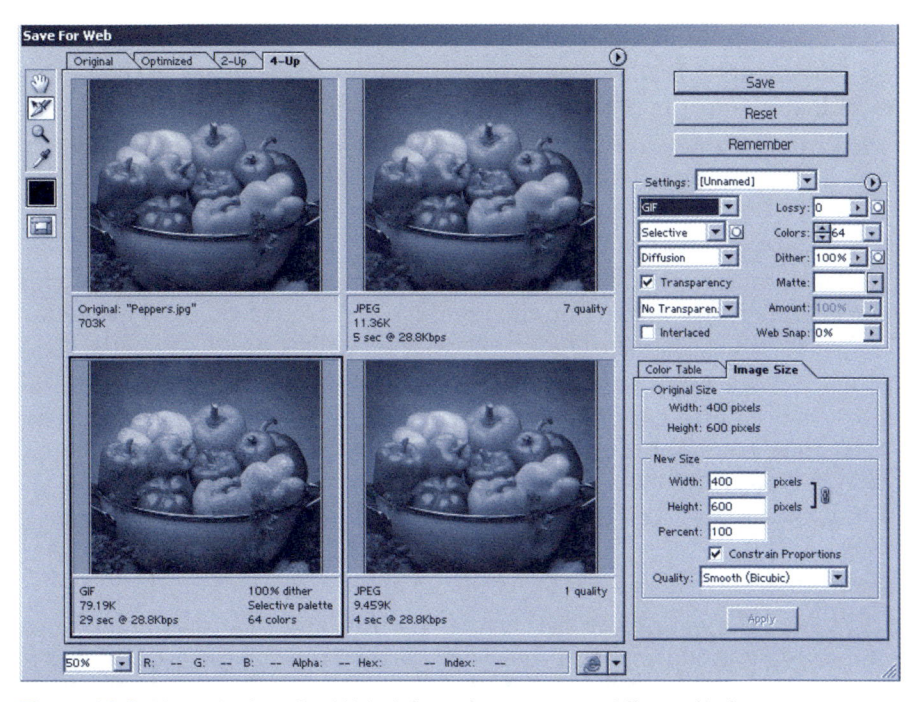

Figure 10.8 Using the Save For Web dialogue box to save in different file formats.

- Choosing **No Dither** applies no dithering to the photo or image.
- Choosing **Diffusion** applies a random pattern of dithering, which is usually less noticeable than the other option, Pattern.

- **Pattern** applies dithering in squares.
- **Noise** also applies a random pattern, but does not show seams in the picture like Diffusion sometimes can.

5. Tick **Transparency** and configure the **Matte** options to make transparent parts of the image actually look transparent, and to blend them in to the picture. Select a matte background color that matches the background of the Web page if necessary.

6. Tick **Interlace** to create a low-resolution image that will come up quickly and remain on the page while the real Web picture is loading. This makes Web pages seem to load faster, but increases the file size.

7. Configure **Web Snap** to specify a tolerance level for shifting colours to the closet Web palette equivalents. Higher values shift more colours. This allows you to use Web-safe colours, and prevents colours from dithering in browsers. More on this in the Appendix.

8. Click on the tab **Image Size**, located next to the Color Table. Here, you can type in new numbers for the size of the image. Click the **Apply** button to see the difference this makes in speed and quality.

9. Manipulate the options to determine the best settings for your picture. Compare download times and the visual display, and use the 4-UP option to view them side by side. Click the **Optimized** tab to see the optimized image.

10. To save the image, press **OK**, and complete the necessary information in the Save Optimized As dialogue box. Rename the image before saving it, if it's from the Samples folder.

There are lots of other things you can do with this dialogue box, but this is a 'simple guide' and our space is limited. While trying to get the most basic terms out there, remember that entire books have been written on optimising files for the Web.

Summary

In this chapter you learned to print images, save images and optimise images for the Web. You also learned about several different file formats, and when they are best used.

Printing in Photoshop 7.0 can be just as simple as printing in any other program, or specialised printing can be done. Specialised prints include printing four-colour separations, camera-ready artwork, printing for spot or process colour, and printing on film and speciality papers such as vellum.

Saving is quite easy too, and is achieved through the Save or Save As dialogue boxes. Saving for the Web is more complicated, and there are multiple options depending on the file type chosen. To optimise before saving, manipulate the settings to decrease file size and maintain colour and quality.

All of these options can be accessed from the File menu.

Appendix

Creating Web pages in Photoshop

Creating a Web page using the Web Photo Gallery command

Summary

Creating Web pages in Photoshop

Photoshop 7.0 enables you to create photo Web galleries quickly and painlessly using the Web Photo Gallery command located under the **File > Automate** menu. Using this command, you can create your own personalised Web page complete with pictures, an e-mail address for contacting you, and even a customised background. All you have to do is gather up your pictures and fill in a little information.

A Web page is a combination of many things: links to other pages, text, pictures, links to e-mail addresses, links to additional information, and so on. You can create a Web page from scratch in Photoshop 7.0 too, and Photoshop allows you to easily create the necessary HTML files as you save your new page. The HTML code tells Web browsers what to do with the components of your website, such as how to load pictures and text, and what to do with the links you've added. For all of you beginners out there, it's best to start with a template, let Photoshop worry about all of that code and stuff, and later you can try creating from scratch. So, gather up some photos along with an idea for a website, and let's get started!

Photoshop just helps you 'create' the Web page; it does not help you upload the page to the Internet. For that, you'll need other software and a company that will host your site.

Creating a Web page using the Web Photo Gallery command

The Web Photo Gallery command offers preconfigured backgrounds, links and automatically generated thumbnails for photographs, and makes creating a Web page as easy as typing in a few words. When you've got an idea and some pictures in mind, you're ready to get started.

To create a website using the Web Photo Gallery command:

1. Create a folder on the hard drive, and name it '*Source*'. Place all of the pictures you want displayed on your website in this folder. Create another folder called '*Destination*'. You'll need both of these folders when using the Web Photo Gallery command.
2. Choose **File > Automate > Web Photo Gallery**. The Web Photo Gallery dialogue box will appear, as shown in Figure A.1.
3. Click on the down arrow next to the word Styles in the site area of the Web Photo Gallery dialogue box. There are several styles of Web pages available. As you click on each one, you'll see a preview on the right. Choose the style that best suits your needs.
4. Type in your e-mail address in the **E-mail** box.
5. Choose an extension .htm or .html.
6. Click the **Browse** button under **Folders** and browse to the location of the folder *Source* that contains the pictures you want to add to this Web page, (see Figure A.2). If there are any subfolders you'd like to include, place a tick in the **Include All Subfolders** checkbox.
7. Click the **Destination** button and browse to the folder *Destination* created in step 1. This is where the destination files will be saved.
8. From the **Options** box, click on the down arrow and choose **Banner** from the drop-down list. Create a site name (the name that will appear on the Web page), type in the name of the photographer, the date and contact info, and select a font.

Really, there isn't much of a difference between .htm and .html. However, the latest conventions tend towards .html, so if you are in doubt, choose this one.

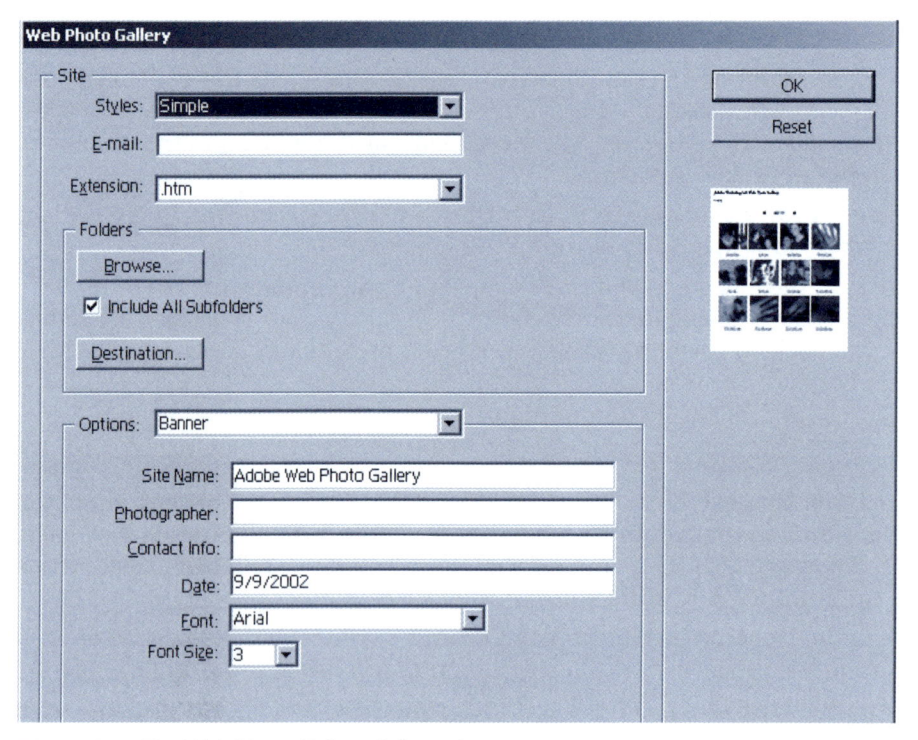

Figure A.1 The Web Photo Gallery dialogue box.

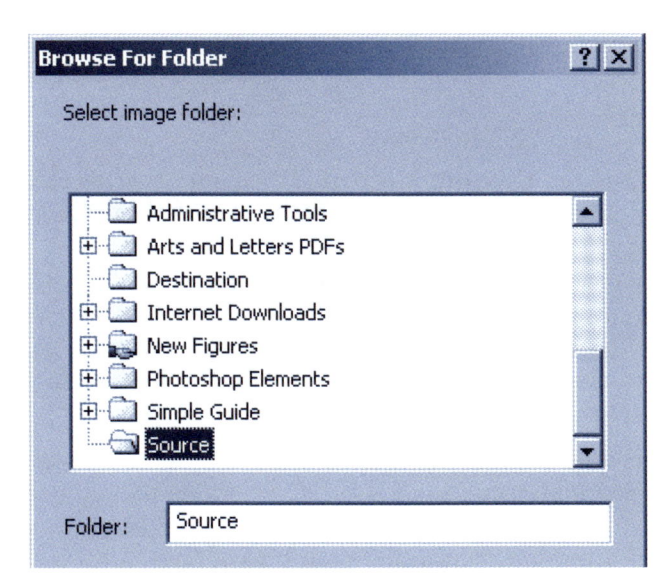

Figure A.2 Browsing to the Source folder.

9. From the **Options** drop-down list, choose **Large Images**. Here, you will configure how the gallery pages should look and how large the images should be. For now, leave **Resize Images** ticked and choose the appropriate file size and quality. It is probably best for now to accept the defaults here; Photoshop knows best!

10. If you want a border around the images, type in a border size. State how you want the file to be named too; I'll stick with *Filename*.

*Locate the folder **Destination**. This folder now contains the .htm or the .html pages you'll need for your website.*

11. From the **Options** drop-down list, choose **Thumbnails**. Here, you will configure how the thumbnail images should look and how large the images should be. For now, accept the defaults. Set a border size, choose how to name the images, and choose a font if desired.
12. From the Options bar, select **Custom Colors**. To change the default colours for Background, Banner, Text, Active Link, Link or Visited Link, click on the colour and change it using the Color Picker.
13. From the **Options** drop-down list, choose **Security**. You can add text to display over your images to prevent theft, show copyright information, and so on. To add custom text or other information, type it here. You can also change the opacity and rotate the text if desired. Experimentation is the key!
14. Click **OK**.
15. The home page will open automatically in your Web browser. After viewing it, you can save the information using the **File > Save As** command. See Figure A3.
16. To edit the pages, choose **File > Automate > Web Photo Gallery** again, and the photo gallery will open for editing.

Summary

In this Appendix, you learned to create a Web page using the Web Photo Gallery command. On this Web page, you can include photographs, text and information about the photographer as well as other information. Using this automated command enables you to create fast and easy Web pages painlessly.

Appendix

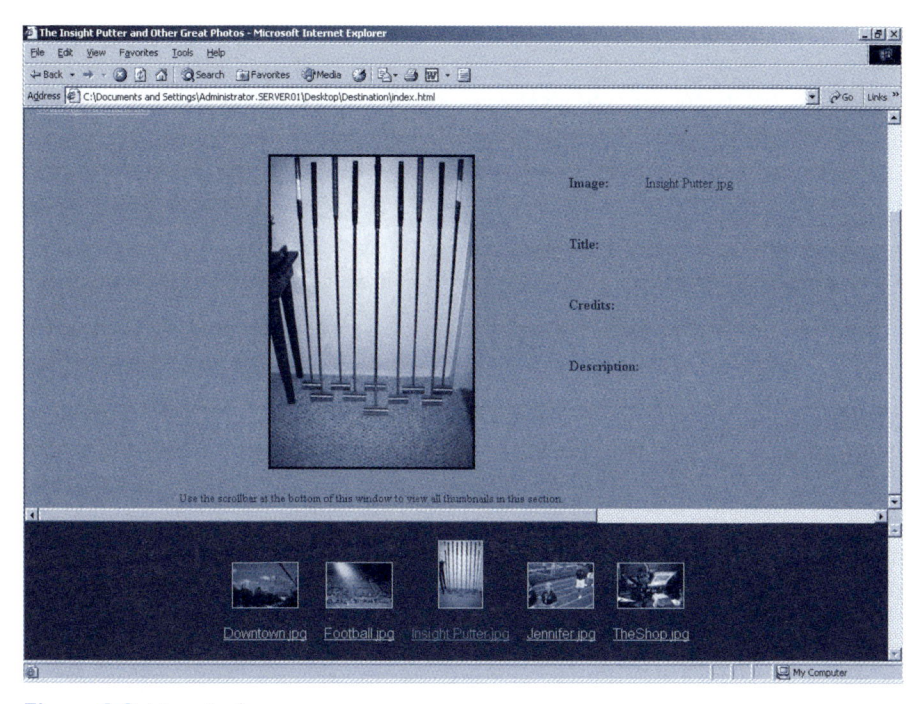

Figure A.3 View the home page.

Index

A
accented edges, 172
Adjustment Layer, 129–31
Airbrush, artwork *see* Brush tool
anchor points, 6, 101, 104, 105, 107
angled strokes, 172
anti-aliasing, type, 153, 156, 157
Artistic filters, 169–73, 184
artwork, 78–97
    background colour, 78–9, 81–4, 88–9
    erasing, 84, 88–90, 91
    foreground, 84, 89
    opening a canvas, 78–9
    setting colours, 80–3
    transparent images, 78–9

B
background, 126, 129, 133, 188
    colour, 69–71, 78–9, 81–4, 88–9
Background eraser, 88, 89
baseline shift, 159, 160
Bevel, 138, 141–2

bitmap format/images, 3, 4, 7, 80
    BMP format, 200, 202
    resizing, 100, 107
    vector reproductions of, 106
blending options, 145–9
blurring images, 61–3, 207
Bounding Box, 106, 114–15, 155
Brightness/Contrast, 36–8, 131
Brush Strokes, 169, 172–3
Brush tools, 21–2, 71, 83–7, 91
    Airbrush, 85, 87
    flow, 85, 87
    options, 11, 20, 84
burning, 63–4, 146

C
camera, connecting, 29–30
caption printing, 191, 192
Character palette, 157–61
circles, drawing, 100, 103–4
Clone Stamp tool, 75–6
CMYK Color, 80, 131
Color Balance, 42–5, 131

Color Overlay, 138
Color Picker, 82, 89, 92, 96, 217
    and type, 154
colour, 15–16, 66–74, 208
    in artwork, 80–3, 89, 92, 96
    AutoColor, 40–2
    and blurring, 62
    Color Balance, 42–5, 131
    Fill layer, 126–9
    and photos, 39–45
    Variations, 43–5
compressing files, 200, 201, 202
contrast, 36–8, 131
copying, 55–6, 117, 120–1
craquelure, 180
cropping, 64–5
curves, drawing, 103–5
Custom shapes tool, 90, 94–5, 107

D
DCS files, 201, 203
Diffusion and web-readying, 208–9
Direct Selection tool, 106–7

distorting images, 59, 60, 61, 173–7
   distorting shapes, 96
   spherize, 174, 175
   twirl, 174, 176
   zig-zag, 174, 177
Dither, 127, 208–9
dodging, 63–4, 146

E
Ellipse tool, 90, 92, 94
emailing images, 200, 201–2, 203–4
embossing, 138, 141–2
EPS files, 201, 203
erasing, 11, 84, 88–90, 91
Eyedropper, 66–8, 70–1, 82, 89, 91

F
Feathering, 74–5
File Browser, 2, 26–8, 29–30
files, 24–6, 35
   creating, 3–4, 5
   formats, 198–203
   optimising for web, 203–4
Fill Layers, 126–9
filters, 168–84
   Artistic, 169–73, 184
   distortion, 173–7
   lighting effects, 177–80
   multiple, 184
   Sketch, 169, 173
   textures, 180–2, 184
   undoing, 173, 174, 182
   and zoom, 182
Find Edges, 179, 181
fonts, 154
foreground, 69–71, 81–3, 107, 116
   artwork, 84, 89
formats, file, 198–203

G
GIF files/format, 200, 201–4, 206
   saving for web, 208–10
glow, 138, 139–41, 173
Glowing Edges, 179, 180
gradient, 126, 127, 131, 138
   Gradient Fill, 126–9
   Gradient tool, 71–4
grain, 173, 180
Grayscale, 80

H
Hand tool, 34, 35
Histogram command, 38
History palette, 15, 16, 18, 45–6
HTML files, 214, 215
hue, 62, 131, 148
   photos, 39–40, 41

I
ICC Profile, 197, 208
ImageReady, 197, 204
images, 28–9, 55–7, 78–97
   blurring, sharpening, smudging, 61–3
   changing colours, 66–74
   Cloning, 75–6
   copying and pasting, 55–6
   cropping, 64–5
   dodging, burning, sponging, 63–4
   feathering, 74–5
   optimising, 35–45
   scale, 58–9
   size, 3–4, 35, 210
   transforming, 58–61
ink outlines, 173
Interlace and web-readying, 210

J
JPEG files/format, 200, 201–2, 203–4
   optimising for web, 206–8

K
kerning, 158–9

L
Lab Color 80
Lasso tools, 53–7, 58, 75
layer masks, 143, 145
Layer Set, 121, 122, 123
layers, 56, 112–24
   adjustment layers, 129–31
   aligning, 132–3
   arranging, 133–5

Index

background, 133
blending options, 145–9
commands, 126–49
copying between, 117, 120–1
creating/destroying, 115–17
distributing, 135
drawing shapes, 102, 103
duplicating, 120–1
Fill Layers, 126–9
grouping, 122
linking, 121–2
locking/unlocking, 118–19, 122
merging, 123, 124
moving, 133–5
Pattern layer, 127
rasterising, 108–9
reducing file size, 124
renaming, 122
showing and hiding, 117
styles, 136–8, 139–44
text, 152
transforming, 58, 63
Layers palette, 13, 16–17, 74, 113–15
applying shadows, 139–41
Blending Options, 146–9
drawing paths, 102
drawing shapes, 92, 95–6
leading, 159, 160
Lens flare effect, 178

levels, adjustment layers, 131
lighting effects, 143, 177–80
directional light, 177
filters, 177–80
focus, 177
global light, 143, 144
luminosity, 62, 148
Line too,l 90, 94
lines, drawing, 83–7, 101–5

M

Magic Eraser, 88, 89–90
Magic Wand, 50–3, 54, 55
Marquee tools, 9, 11, 65, 74, 75
Matte, 208, 210
Mosaic Tiles, 181, 182, 183
Move tool, 10, 133–5

N

Navigator palette, 15, 16–17, 18, 32
negative/s, 45, 131, 191
Noise, 141, 210

O

opacity, 116, 129, 184
drawing lines, 84, 87
optimising for web, 203–10, 211

P

Paint Bucket, 68–71, 72, 91, 116
paintbrush, 85–7
painting effects, 169–73
Palette Knife, 170, 172

Palette Well, 8, 13, 18–20, 28
palettes, 13–18
moving, 16, 18–20
Options Bar, 19–22
resizing, 16–17, 18
Paragraph palette, 157, 160–1
Paragraph Type, 154–5
pasting images, 55–7
Path Selection tool, 105–6, 107
paths, 6, 101–5
aligning, 106
defined, 5–6, 100
editing, 106–7
modifying, 100–9
rasterising, 107–9
Pattern layer, 127
Pattern Overlay, 138
Pattern and saving for web, 210
PDF files, 201, 203
Pen tool, 6, 100, 105
drawing paths, 101–5
Options bar, 101–3
Pencil tool, 83–5
perspective, 59–60, 61, 96
Photographic Effects, 139
photonegatives, 45
photos, 3–4, 143
brightness, 36–8
and colour, 39–45

Index

Photos (Continued)
  contrast, 36–8
  editing, 50–76, 97
    Lasso tool, 53–7, 58
    Magic Wand, 50–3, 54, 55
  enhancing, 24–47
  Open command, 24–6
  resizing and zooming, 30–5
  using File Browser, 26–8
PICT format, 200, 202
Point Type, 154–5
Polygon tool, 90, 94
printing, 4, 186–95
  background, 188
  bleed, 190
  calibration bars, 191, 193
  caption, 191, 192
  crop marks, 191, 193
  emulsion down, 191
  encoding, 192
  interpolation, 191
  labels, 191
  negative, 191
  options, 186
  page set-up, 186–8, 194
  preview, 188
  Print dialogue box, 188–93, 194, 195
  printer properties, 195
  registration marks, 191, 193
  screen, 190
  setting Print Options, 193
  transfer, 190
PSD files, 201, 203

R

rasterising, 107–9
  type, 153, 164–5
Rectangle tools, 90, 92
relief, 182
Reset tool, 12, 64
resizing, 31–5, 58–9, 61, 100
  for web, 206–7, 216
resolution, 4, 78
RGB Color, 79, 80, 85, 131
rotating images, 59, 60–1, 96

S

Satin, 138
saturation, 39–40, 62, 131, 148
Save As dialogue box, 195–7
Save for Web command, 204–10
saving, 34, 195–7
  file formats, 198–203
  photos, 45–7
  setting preferences, 198, 199
  shapes, 102, 107
  snapshots, 45–6
  using filters, 183
  for web, 203–10, 211
scale, 58–9, 96, 161
scanner images, 28–9

Selective Color, 131
shadows, 138, 139–41
Shape tool, 70, 92–3, 105
shapes, 90, 91–7, 102–5
  adjusting size, 95–7
  colour, 95, 96
  distorting, 96
  editing, 96–7
  New Shape Layer, 103
  Options bar, 90, 92, 93–4
  perspective, 96
  rasterising, 108–9
  rotate, 96
  saving, 107
  scale, 96
  skewing, 96
  transforming, 96–7
  see also paths
sharpening images, 61–3
size, 3–4, 35, 207
  file, 3–4, 5, 35
  of shapes, 95–7
Sketch filters, 169, 173
skewing, 59, 60, 61, 96
  type, 161
smudging images, 61–3
snapshots, saving, 45–6
spatter, 173
speech bubbles, 94
sponging, 63–4

Index

Spotlight, 177, 178
Stained Glass, 181
Stroke, 138
Styles, 93
    layer, 136–8, 139–44
Swatches, 82

T

text *see* type
textures, 180–2, 184
thumbnails, 26–7, 218
TIFF files/format, 200, 201–3, 206
Tolerance, 51, 71, 89
Toolbox, 7–10, 20–1
    hidden tools, 7
    and Layers palette, 114
    resetting, 12
tracking, 159, 160

transparency, 78–9, 210
type, 152–65
    aligning options, 156
    anti-aliasing, 153, 156, 157
    Character palette, 157–61
    flip, 161
    Paragraph palette, 157, 160–1
    Paragraph and Point, 154–5
    rasterising, 153, 164–5
    scale, 161
    skewing, 161
    Type tools, 11, 13, 152–4
    warping, 161–4

U

undoing, 15, 16, 45
    filters, 173, 174, 182

V

Variations command, 43–5
vector images, 5–6, 7, 107, 108
    rasterising, 108–9

W

Water Paper filter, 173, 174
watercolour effects, 169–73
web pages, creating, 214–18
Web Photo Gallery, 214–18
Web Snap, 210
web-readying files, 203–10

Z

Zoom tool, 30–4, 182

For where to go, who to read and what to know in the world of IT.

If you're looking for books on IT then visit: **www.it-minds.com**, the place where you can find books from the IT industry's leading IT publishers.

[Choice of publishers]

IT-Minds is home to some of the world's leading computer book publishers such as Sams, Que, Addison-Wesley, Prentice Hall, Adobe Press, Peachpit Press, Cisco Press and Macromedia Press.

[Choice of ways to learn]

We publish for those who are completely new to a computer through to the most cutting-edge technologies for the IT professional and our products offer a variety of ways to learn. IT-Minds offers you tutorials, handy pocket guides, comprehensive references, exam guides, CD based training materials and Executive Briefings.

[Choice of subjects]

We also cover the A-Z of computer subjects: From ASP, Bluetooth, C++, Database, E-Mail, Flash, Graphics, HTML ... to Windows XP, XML, Yahoo and Zope.

Infinite choices for the IT Minded

As an IT mind you also have access to:
- News from the IT industry
- Free weekly newsletters
- Articles written by our featured authors
- Competitions to win prizes
- Testing and assessment products
- Online IT training products

[Custom Solutions]

If you found this book useful, then so might your colleagues or customers. If you would like to explore corporate purchases or custom editions personalised with your brand or message, then just get in touch at **www.it-minds.com/corporate.asp**

Visit our website at: **[www.it-minds.com]**